AN ECONOMETRIC MODEL
OF
THE UNITED STATES, 1929–1952

CONTRIBUTIONS
TO
ECONOMIC ANALYSIS

IX

EDITED BY
J. TINBERGEN
P. J. VERDOORN
H. J. WITTEVEEN

1964
NORTH-HOLLAND PUBLISHING COMPANY
AMSTERDAM

AN ECONOMETRIC MODEL

OF

THE UNITED STATES

1929-1952

BY

L. R. KLEIN

AND

A. S. GOLDBERGER

1964
NORTH-HOLLAND PUBLISHING COMPANY
AMSTERDAM

Second Printing 1964

Printed in the Netherlands

INTRODUCTION TO THE SERIES

This series consists of a number of hitherto unpublished studies. They are introduced by the editors in the belief that they represent fresh contributions to economic science.

The term *economic analysis* as used in the title of the series has been adopted because it covers both the activities of the theoretical economist and of the research worker.

Although the analytical methods used by the various contributors are not the same, they are nevertheless conditioned by the common origin of their studies, namely theoretical problems encountered in practical research. Since for this reason, business cycle research and national accounting, research work on behalf of economic policy, and problems of planning are the main sources of the subjects dealt with, they necessarily determine the manner of approach adopted by the authors. Their methods tend to be "practical" in the sense of not being too far remote from application to actual economic conditions. In addition they are quantitative rather than qualitative.

It is the hope of the editors that the publication of these studies will help to stimulate the exchange of scientific information and to reinforce international cooperation in the field of economics.

THE EDITORS

PREFACE

As seems inevitable in economic research with contemporary statistical series, past results become quickly modified by revisions of the data. After having spent more than three years at work on the econometric model construction described in this book, we now find ourselves outdated by the basic revisions of the national income accounts made by the U.S. Department of Commerce in mid-summer 1954. In problems of both basic model construction and current, short run forecasts we have managed to deal adequately with the type of data revision which takes place regularly – that which transforms preliminary estimates of statistical series into final figures. However, we are dealing now with a more comprehensive revision which affects data for many years past. The level of gross national product, the factorial distribution of national income, and other important aspects of the social accounts have been changed.

We mention this because it has been our objective in this volume to present an up-to-date econometric model of the United States which others could apply to practical economic problems akin to those in business cycle forecasting, which we exemplify at some length in the text. While we feel that the models presented give empirical insight into the structure of the United States economy, we caution the reader who would, in the future, try to use it for forecasting as we have done in 1953 and 1954. Even if the problem of comprehensive data revision were not present, we would still recommend re-estimation of parameters by extending the sample period beyond 1952 before using the model for problems in 1955 and thereafter. The recent data changes simply make the problem of parameter re-estimation more urgent.

As a minimal guide to the future use of the models already estimated, we present a table of residuals for 1949–54, i.e. of differences between actual values of the main endogenous variables and those estimated by the structural equations when observed values of the "explanatory variables" are inserted. The recently revised data are used in all these calculations which are made for the system estimated through 1952.

Year	Consumption equation	Investment equation	Corporate savings equation	Relation of corporate profits to nonwage nonfarm income	Depreciation equation
1949	0.0	−6.2	1.1	0.1	−1.1
1950	0.5	3.4	0.0	0.6	−0.2
1951	−2.3	2.5	0.2	0.7	−0.8
1952	−1.7	2.2	0.2	−0.2	0.0
1953	−2.1	0.1	0.1	−0.8	0.5
1954*	−3.8	−2.4	−0.2	−1.6	1.6

Year	Labor demand equation	Production function	Wage adjustment equation	Import demand equation
1949	−1.1	−4.3	−3.4	−0.1
1950	1.7	0.1	−3.5	0.8
1951	1.1	−0.3	6.8	0.0
1952	2.2	0.3	−7.5	0.4
1953	4.4	3.3	0.6	0.5
1954*	2.3	1.6	−6.8	−0.1

Year	Farm income equation	Relation of agricultural to nonagricultural prices
1949	−0.3	−34
1950	0.0	−33
1951	−0.1	−17
1952	−0.5	−38
1953	−1.0	−75
1954*	−1.2	−82

Because these calculations were prepared expressly for the purpose of forecasting economic activity in 1955, they do not cover four of the structural equations, those dealing with money and interest rates, which are not needed for forecasts one year in advance. As can be seen from the table of residuals, four of the equations appear to have a definite

* Data for 1954 are preliminary.

bias in recent years, when the new data are used. These are the consumption equation, the labor demand equation, the farm income equation, and the relation between farm and nonfarm prices. Even with the old data, the last-mentioned equation and probably the penultimate also would show biased residuals for recent years. In any event, for a simple and crude adjustment, one using our model should add the 1954 residuals to the constant term of these four particular equations.

Since no official national income data on the old basis were published for the entire calendar year 1954, we feel compelled to furnish the reader with grounds for judging the accuracy or realization of our 1954 forecast [1]). We shall compare the actual change between 1953

Review of 1954 Forecasts

Variable	Actual Change 1953 to 1954*	Forecast Change December 1953	Forecast Change June 1954**
Gross National Product, $Y + T + D$	\$ $-$ 4.6 billion	\$ $-$ 5.3 billion	\$ $-$ 5.5 billion
Consumption, C	0.8	1.2	0.7
Investment, I	$-$ 2.7	$-$ 3.3	$-$ 2.6
Imports, F_I	$-$ 0.3	$-$ 0.2	0.0
Private Employee Compensation, W_1	$-$ 1.2	$-$ 2.4	$-$ 2.3
Nonwage nonfarm income, P	$-$ 1.8	$-$ 0.1	0.2
Agricultural income, A_1	$-$ 0.2	0.5	0.8
Depreciation, D	1.1	$-$ 2.6	$-$ 2.2
Employment, N_W	$-$ 0.9 million persons	$-$ 0.3 million persons	$-$ 0.9 million persons
Price level, p	0.3 index points	16.1 index points	14.2 index points
Wage rate, w	10.9	18.1	18.4

[1]) This forecast was orginally presented at a conference on the analysis of the economic outlook at the University of Michigan in November, 1953. It was presented to a wider audience, in a slightly improved form, through publication in *The Manchester Guardian Weekly*, January 7, 1954, p. 3.

* The 1954 data used are preliminary.

** In June 1954 we prepared a mid-year revision of our annual forecast, taking into account changes in estimates of predetermined variables since the December 1953 forecasts. This mid-year forecast was summarized for the record in *The New York Times*, July 5, 1954, p. 18.

and 1954, calculated on the new basis, for the endogenous variables of the model, with the change between the 1953 values assumed at the time of forecast and the forecast 1954 values. We thus compare actual year-to-year change with the forecasted change.

For the main and important variables these forecasts are close to reality. A principal discrepancy is in the overestimation of price increase, a tendency in our model of which we were quite aware at the time of forecast. In preparing the mid-year revision for 1954, we noted that an upward shift of the production function to allow for a more than linear trend growth in productivity would imply a considerably reduced degree of price increase.

We must point out that some of the assumptions made regarding predetermined variables in December 1953 and in June 1954 were not actually realized in 1954. Our main assumptions about fiscal legislation were qualitatively correct but government expenditures, in current dollars, were assumed at an excessively high level. Instead of the $ 6.5 billion reduction which actually occurred, our December and June forecasts assumed $ 1.2 billion and $ 1.6 billion reductions respectively. On the other hand, instead of the actual 0.1 billion current dollar reduction in compensation of government employees our forecasts assumed $ 0.6 billion and $ 0.4 billion reductions. Instead of the actual 0.7 billion current dollar increase in exports, our forecasts assumed a $ 2.3 billion increase and a $ 0.4 billion decrease respectively. Hours worked declined by 3% rather than by the 1% postulated in both our forecasts. Our assumptions on the size of population, labor force, government employees, farmers, and nonfarm entrepreneurs were virtually identical with actual 1954 values. The indexes of import prices and agricultural exports each rose by 7 points, contrasted with our "no-change" assumptions.

Estimates of lagged variables which entered into our forecasts were based upon preliminary and unrevised data. Revised calculations show that the only significant discrepancy was in the lagged wage rate index, which actually rose by 19.0 points rather than the assumed 23.5 points (December) or 25.1 points (June). Finally, it may be noted that in reference to constant dollar government expenditures, our overestimate of the current dollar value was counteracted by our overestimation of the endogenous price level increase. On balance, the actual $ 3.4 billion reduction in real government expenditures compared with estimates of a $ 3.7 billion reduction (December) and a $ 2.7 billion reduction (June).

We cannot embark upon our research story without giving due acknowledgment to the many people who assisted us greatly. The entire work was done as a project of the Research Seminar in Quantitative Economics of the University of Michigan. At an early stage many economists were invited to comment on the nature of the proposed model. From sources too numerous to mention by name, many helpful suggestions were received. On problems of data collection and preparation we received indispensable aid from Karl Fox, Lenore Frane, Irwin Friend, Raymond Goldsmith, George Jaszi, and Homer Jones. Bruce Arden provided great assistance in programming our calculations on an electronic computing machine, and Stefan Valavanis-Vail also helped with this aspect of our work. Our colleague, Richard Musgrave, generously gave us expert advice on fiscal policies used in forecasting and in our general analytical work. For manuscript preparation we are indebted to Courtney Sherbrooke Adams, Katherine Craig, and Barbara Cromarty.

Oxford, England   *L. R. K. and A. S. G.*
Ann Arbor, Michigan, U.S.A.
   January 1955

CONTENTS

I. INTRODUCTION 1
   Historical Notes 1
   Lessons from Experience 2

II. DISCUSSION OF THE MODEL 4
   The Consumption Equation 4
   The Investment Equation 10
   The Corporate Savings Equation 13
   The Relation between Corporate Profits and Nonwage Nonfarm Income 14
   The Depreciation Equation 15
   The Demand for Labor Equation. 16
   The Production Function 17
   The Labor Market Adjustment Equation 18
   The Import Demand Equation. 19
   The Agricultural Income Determination Equation 20
   The Relation between Agricultural and Nonagricultural Prices . . . 22
   The Household Liquidity Preference Equation 23
   The Business Liquidity Preference Equation. 26
   The Relation between Short and Long Term Interest Rates 28
   The Money Market Adjustment Equation 29
   Definitions and Accounting Identities. 31

III. SOME PROPERTIES OF THE SYSTEM 34

IV. STATISTICAL ESTIMATION OF THE MODEL 42
   Methods. 42
   Empirical Results 50
   Remarks on the Consumption Equation. 57
   Remarks on the Investment Equation 66
   Remarks on the Relation between Corporate Profits and Nonwage Non-
     farm Income and on the Depreciation Equation 68
   Remarks on the Production Function. 69
   Remarks on the Agricultural Income Determination Equation 69
   Remarks on the Household and Business Liquidity Preference Equations 70
   Note on Computational Methods 70

V. EXTRAPOLATION AND FORECASTING 72
   Some Principles of Forecasting. 72
   Extrapolations of the Model to 1951 and 1952 78
   Forecasts for 1953 82

VI.   Revision of the Model and Forecasts for 1954   89
      Revision of the Model.   89
      Forecasts for 1954   95
      Two-Year Multipliers   112

Appendix I   The Basic Time Series   115
      General Comments   115
      Income and Product Flows   115
      Personal Tax-Transfer Items.   116
      Stock of Capital   117
      Liquid Asset Holdings   117
      Sources of Data for Sample Period   118
      Sources of Data   118
      Sample Data.   131
      Sources of Data for Extrapolation and Forecasting.   133
      Extrapolations to 1951 and 1952   134
      Forecasts for 1953   135
      Forecasts for 1954   136

Appendix II   The Tax-Transfer Functions   142
      Introduction   142
      Forecasts for 1954   143
      Indirect Taxes Less Subsidies   143
      Taxes less Transfers on Wage Income.   145
      Corporate Income and Excess Profits Taxes   147
      Taxes less Transfers on Personal Nonwage Nonfarm Income   149
      Taxes less Transfers on Farm Income.   151
      Forecasts for 1953   152
      Indirect Taxes Less Subsidies   152
      Taxes Less Transfers on Wage Income   152
      Corporate Income and Excess Profits Taxes   153
      Taxes Less Transfers on Nonwage Nonfarm Income   153
      Taxes Less Transfers on Farm Income   154
      Tax-Transfer Functions for Calculation of Two-Year Multipliers . . .   154

Appendix III   Residuals from Estimated Equations.   156

EXPLANATION OF SYMBOLS

$Y + T + D$	Gross national product, 1939 dollars
C	Consumer expenditures, 1939 dollars
I	Gross private domestic capital formation, 1939 dollars
G	Government expenditures for goods and services, 1939 dollars
p	Price index of gross national product, 1939: 100
F_E	Exports of goods and services, 1939 dollars
F_I	Imports of goods and services, 1939 dollars
W_1	Private employee compensation, deflated
W_2	Government employee compensation, deflated
P	Nonwage nonfarm income, deflated
A_1	Farm income, deflated
A_2	Government payments to farmers, deflated
$A_1 + A_2 = A$	Total farm income, deflated
D	Capital consumption charges, 1939 dollars
P_C	Corporate profits, deflated
S_P	Corporate savings, deflated
T	Indirect taxes less subsidies, deflated
T_W	Personal and payroll taxes less transfers associated with wage and salary income, deflated
T_P	Personal and corporate taxes less transfers associated with nonwage nonfarm income, deflated
T_C	Corporate income taxes, deflated
T_A	Taxes less transfers associated with farm income, deflated
B	End-of-year corporate surplus, deflated, from arbitrary origin
K	End-of-year stock of private capital, 1939 dollars, from arbitrary origin
F_A	Index of agricultural exports, 1939: 100
p_A	Index of agricultural prices, 1939: 100

p_1	Index of prices of imports, 1939: 100
N_P	Number of persons in the United States
N	Number of persons in the labor force
N_W	Number of wage- and salary-earners
N_G	Number of government employees
N_F	Number of farm operators
N_E	Number of nonfarm entrepreneurs
h	Index of hours worked per year, 1939: 1.00
w	Index of hourly wages, 1939: 122.1
i_L	Average yield on corporate bonds
i_S	Average yield on short term commercial paper
R	Excess reserves of banks as a percentage of total reserves
L_1	End-of-year liquid assets held by persons, deflated
L_2	End-of-year liquid assets held by businesses, deflated
t	Time trend, years, from arbitrary origin

I. INTRODUCTION

A fresh attempt, drawing upon recent research developments, has been made, and described in these pages, at constructing an econometric model of the United States. A distinctive feature of the present research is that the task is not being viewed as a "once-and-for-all" job. The research described here is part of a more continuous program in that new data, reformulations, and extrapolations are constantly being studied. As new observations or revised observations become available, the parameters of the model are re-estimated. As a result of forecasting experience and the acquisition of other a priori information, the equations are restructured. Moreover, intensive econometric investigations are currently being made of particular sectors, partially in the hope of improving the general model described here. These sector studies include the construction industry, foreign trade, agriculture, and the money market. They are not, however, at a stage of completion allowing incorporation in this volume.

The first comprehensive model of the United States economy, as we all know, is the time honored study of Tinbergen [1]) for the League of Nations. Since the date of his study, the basic time series data of the United States have been drastically revised. In addition, various theoretical discussions have led in recent years to some reformulations of the underlying model. The study by one of the present authors [2]) for the Cowles Commission was an attempt to carry on from Tinbergen's great start with newer data and newer theoretical ideas.

Both of these models, covering only the period before World War II, are quite inadequate in the present situation. Moreover, conditions are such that it would be inefficient simply to extend either of them mecha-

---

[1]) J. Tinbergen, *Statistical Testing of Business Cycle Theories*, II, *Business Cycles in the United States of America, 1919–1932*, (Geneva: League of Nations, 1939).

[2]) L. R. Klein, *Economic Fluctuations in the United States, 1921–1941*. (New York: John Wiley and Sons, 1950).

nically to the present period with data adjusted to the conceptual basis used in these older studies. For a variety of purposes, Christ [1]) has extended the prewar models to 1946 and 1947, but his results are in many ways unsatisfactory.

The only case known to the authors of a continuous econometric project of the type discussed here is that reported by Brown [2]) of the Canadian government. He describes econometric model building in Canada in terms of continuous refinement of data, re-estimation of parameters, testing forecasts, and revising equations over a period of several years. In many respects, the present model for the United States will draw upon the Canadian research.

LESSONS FROM EXPERIENCE

Using some cruder interpretations of macroeconomic structure derived from the Keynesian theory of employment, the prewar model prepared at the Cowles Commission gave inadequate treatment to prices and wages, both absolute and real.

The postwar inflation showed this deficiency in a striking manner; hence the present model attempts to give superior treatment to this aspect of the system. The high level of postwar consumption is another event which showed up defects in previous models. The production process was hidden in this prewar model, but is introduced explicitly in the present scheme. As a result of attempts to improve the model in these few respects, other changes will be needed in order to retain completeness of the system. This will all be explained as we work our way through the system equation by equation.

In 1951, the basic data gathering agency in the United States, the National Income Division of the Department of Commerce, thoroughly revised the national accounts [3]). The new econometric

---

[1]) C. Christ, "A Test of an Econometric Model for the United States, 1921–1947," *Conference on Business Cycles*, (New York: National Bureau of Economic Research, 1951).

[2]) T. M. Brown, "Canadian Experience in Forecasting from Econometric Models." Delivered at the Meetings of the Econometric Society, December, 1951 (Unpublished).

[3]) *National Income and Product of the United States, 1929–1950*, prepared by the National Income Division, U.S. Department of Commerce, Washington, D.C., 1951. Supplement to the *Survey of Current Business*.

model estimated here will rest essentially on the foundation provided by these data. Except in cases particularly noted, we shall adhere to the concepts of the Department of Commerce. One of their most valuable new contributions for our purposes is the preparation of a set of constant dollar estimates of gross national product and its main components. We shall try to achieve a very specific blending of real and money values in our model and will need to rely heavily on their estimates of constant dollar magnitudes, with associated price deflators. Their data extend backwards in time only to 1929. Rather than adopt an imperfect splicing carrying us back to 1919, we have deemed it advisable to use no data prior to 1929, except for estimates of initial values in equations with time lags. We shall strive for a more refined model in the matter of basic data.

Another front on which recent advances have been made is computational technique. Modern econometric methods call for a much heavier computational burden than heretofore experienced. We shall draw upon efficient designs developed at the Cowles Commission for estimation of parameters in equation systems and upon the use of higher speed computing machines. The latter devices permit much more experimentation and repeated estimation under new circumstances than would otherwise have been possible. In fact, modern machine methods hold much promise for more powerful analyses than we have been able to carry out to date. In a modest and preliminary way we have used electronic equipment for the present study, but in our continuing research program, we constantly look forward to greater use of high speed machines to enable us to attack otherwise unmanageable econometric problems [1]).

---

[1]) See p. 70 below.

II. DISCUSSION OF THE MODEL

THE CONSUMPTION EQUATION

In structural estimation of an econometric model we are interested in describing actions or behavior of particular human beings in each relationship of the system. In the consumption equation, we are interested in describing the behavior of households as consumers, i.e. as people who demand goods and services from the market.

The simplest type of consumption function that we derive from models of Keynesian economics is a linear relation between consumer expenditures and income. Perhaps both variables may be corrected for price changes. However, what appears to be a stable relationship fitted to the data of the prewar period does not carry over well into the postwar years. The prewar, linear consumption-income relations seriously underestimate postwar expenditures, and even recomputation with postwar observations will not lead us to a satisfactory estimate for the present model.

One of the most frequently discussed exceptions to the linear relation between aggregate consumption and aggregate income is the effect of income distribution. Students of family budget data have often pointed out the non-linearity of Engel curves for types of household spending. Postwar surveys of consumers in the United States are particularly illuminating since they include relatively more high income recipients than do other surveys. The striking nonlinearities in the consumption-income relation, evidences of income distribution effects, are found only if the high groups are included. In Figure 1, we see the increase in the slope of the savings-income relation as we move up the income scale.

Characteristics of the size distribution of income would be desirable variables in an aggregative consumption function, but unfortunately such data are lacking on a continuous basis for all but the postwar years.

The national income statistics of the United States do, however,

4

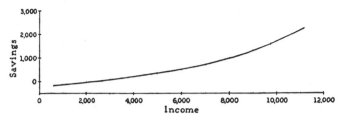

Fig. 1. Mean Savings and Mean Disposable Income by Classes of
Disposable Income
(Nonfarm, Nonbusiness Spending Units in the United States 1948–1950)

Source: Unpublished tabulations from the data collected in the *Surveys of Consumer Finances*. Savings instead of consumption are dealt with as the dependent variable since savings are *directly* estimated in the *Surveys*. Consumption is a residual estimate.

provide a continuous flow of data since 1929 on the functional distribution of income, i.e. the distribution among wages and salaries, entrepreneurial income, farm income, dividends, rent, interest, and other such types. An income distribution phenomenon found in Kalecki's [1]) business-cycle theory and in various other schemes is a linear consumption function dependent on two separate variables, wage and nonwage income. Insofar as wage income corresponds to low income and nonwage income to high income, we have an approximation to the effects of the size distribution of income. If the true situation were as depicted in Figure 2, we would have two linear segments pieced together in a trivariate linear relation to approximate a single bivariate nonlinear relation.

We know, in fact, that the aggregative statistics on wages and other income types are heterogeneous and do not provide a clear distinction between high and low income persons. Corporation executives with high salaries are included among wage earners, while small shopkeepers with low incomes are included in the nonwage group. Moreover, many people get both types of income simultaneously.

Even though the above considerations obscure the separate effects of wage and nonwage income, there is a basic reason why the distinction between wage and nonwage income is of importance in the consumption

---

[1]) M. Kalecki, "A Macrodynamic Theory of Business Cycles," *Econometrica*, Vol. III, 1935, pp. 327–44.

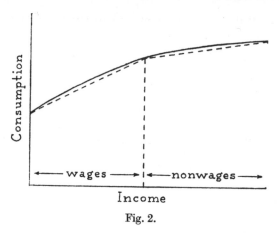

Fig. 2.

equation of our model. Owners of unincorporated enterprise, professional workers, and artisans lead joint financial lives as producers and
consumers. Their incomes and their savings are partly personal and
partly business. In the national income accounts, there is no way of
distinguishing between business and personal savings of these people.
They tend to show higher marginal saving rates out of income than
do wage earners, since they have immediately evident investment
outlets for their accumulated savings. In addition, the difficulties of
raising loan funds in modern capital markets have pushed these people
towards heavier reliance on retained earnings. The Surveys of Consumer
Finances indicate in postwar years that businessmen are relatively
high savers and that the principal reason for this is the high rate of retention of income in business [1]).

High marginal saving propensities are observed among farmers as
well as among businessmen. Prewar sample surveys were able to
distinguish between the savings-income patterns of farmers and other
consumers. They show the same result as the postwar surveys. In the
case of farmers, besides the incentive to save for ploughing back funds
into productive resources, there is the influence of the rural way
of life with comparatively fewer expenditure outlets for consumer items.

[1]) See J. N. Morgan, "The Structure of Aggregate Personal Saving," *The Journal
of Political Economy*, Vol. LIX, 1951, pp. 528–534. L. R. Klein and J. Margolis,
"Statistical Studies of Unincorporated Business," *The Review of Economics and
Statistics*, Vol. XXXVI, 1954, pp. 33–46.

Thus we shall find it convenient and useful to build three income types linearly into our consumption function. These are wage income with the highest marginal propensity to consume, nonwage nonfarm income with the next highest marginal propensity to consume, and farm income with the smallest marginal propensity to consume.

Disposable income is generally recognized as the appropriate variable for equations of consumer demand. National income, as a specific concept, does not take account of tax payments and transfers, flows of major importance in the United States. Statistical estimates of total disposable income are available in the national income accounts as are estimates of the main factor shares of total national income. Series of disposable income by factor shares were not available in this country [1]; therefore special estimates for the purpose of constructing the model at hand were prepared [2].

The definition of total disposable income used by the Department of Commerce regards corporate savings as a flow of funds unavailable for personal expenditures. We have accordingly subtracted corporate savings from nonwage, nonfarm income in the process of getting disposable factor shares. This particular treatment is debatable in the sense that shareholders may feel more opulent if the companies in which they own shares are accumulating profits. If one were to pursue this matter further, he would also conclude that other capital gains, an important variable in Tinbergen's model of the U.S. economy, should also be included in disposable income. On other occasions, statistical tests have not revealed much importance of capital gains, especially when the sample is not dominated by the 1920's.

We have regarded the practices of the Department of Commerce as the most realistic in the study of consumer behavior and have excluded corporate savings from nonwage, nonfarm disposable income. As will be seen below we do not make a similar exclusion in the investment equation; hence, we shall have need for explicit study of corporate

---

[1] The econometric models of Canada have, for many years, made use of separate series on disposable wage and disposable nonwage income. See T. M. Brown, "Habit Persistence and Lags in Consumer Behavior," *Econometrica*, Vol. 20, 1952, pp. 355–371.

[2] Lenore Frane and L. R. Klein, "The Estimation of Disposable Income by Distributive Shares," *The Review of Economics and Statistics*, Vol. XXXV, 1953, pp. 333–37.

savings behavior. Specifications like these are important in identifying the statistical relations we estimate as structural patterns of behavior.

Modifications in the simplest version of the Keynesian consumption functions have thus been suggested to take account of income distribution, taxes, and transfer payments. Another familiar variation on the standard version of this equation is that concerning the influence of the past, or lags in behavior. It is generally recognized that consumers do not react immediately to changes in income; hence, some lagged, as well as current, values of income are used as variables. In our model, the influence of the past on present consumer behavior will be represented by lagged consumption, not lagged income. Our hypothesis will be that consumer behavior tends to be repetitive to some extent, but that adjustments will be made in accordance with the income situation and other variables [1]).

A more basic modification of the Keynesian theory has been the argument that wealth variables should be in the consumption function. We introduce a wealth variable in the form of beginning-of-period liquid assets held by households. It may be thought that liquid assets do not give a true picture of the wealth status as it should be measured in the consumption function. But liquid assets are a strategic form of wealth, as far as consumer behavior is concerned. They are the money balances that are spent for goods and services. Other consumer assets are not as easily convertible into a spendable form, although this remark applies differently among the various assets held by households. At the individual level, liquid assets are highly correlated with overall consumer wealth, and thus serve as a good wealth indicator. Liquid assets are far easier to measure than most other consumer assets and provide a fairly reliable series. Wealth statistics are not generally of high accuracy. Studies of individual families in cross section samples from consumer surveys bear out the comparative importance of liquid assets as opposed to debt variables [2]).

---

[1]) See T. M. Brown, *op. cit.*

[2]) L. R. Klein, "Assets, Debts and Economic Behavior," *Studies in Income and Wealth*, Vol. XIV, (New York: National Bureau of Economic Research, 1951), pp. 195–227. In some more recent studies of durable goods purchases, based on data collected in the 1952 and 1953 Surveys of Consumer Finances, debt appears to be more significantly related to purchases than do liquid asset holdings.

In a general theory of consumer planning over time, initial stocks of wealth enter as variables in demand functions derived from some theory of behavior such as, e.g., utility maximization. If we regard the consumer as periodically revising the time shape of future plans, we shall obtain a dynamic equation of actual (not simply planned) demand dependent on the wealth in existence at the beginning of each period. In our statistical analysis, the basic period is one year, and this may be too long for the dynamics of consumer planning, but it is this type of reasoning that leads us to make the convenient assumption that beginning-of-period assets influence consumer expenditures of each period. It will be seen later that this assumption simplifies some of our estimation problems since liquid assets are classified as a predetermined variable in the consumption equation.

If the wealth concept is to be expanded beyond the variable now used, liquid assets, we shall probably want to consider stocks of consumer durables. These are undoubtedly of some significance in explaining the transition from war to postwar spending. In the present aggregative model, consumer durables are not treated apart from nondurables, but in a less aggregative model making the distinction between the two types of goods, the stock of durables will undoubtedly be in the system.

The final variable appearing in our consumption function is total population. We could use per capita variables instead of an explicit population variable, but this would raise a problem as to the measurement of wage income per person. The same is true of farm and nonfarm nonwage income. Since some people get many types of income, as noted above, separate population deflators for each factor share are not entirely satisfactory.

Other demographic variables may eventually be considered for inclusion in future models. Average family size, average age, and racial composition of the population are all plausible, although several slowly moving trends of these types will certainly be highly intercorrelated. The urban-rural population composition is often mentioned as of importance, but we extract the influence of such a variable already by our separate treatment of farm income.

Our consumption equation is a "real" equation. Consumer expenditures are measured in 1939 dollars, and income flows and liquid assets are deflated by the general price index. It may be argued that deflation in the consumption equation by the price of consumer goods would be preferable, but we defer to a later more complex model the problem of estimating systems with several endogenous price levels.

The considerations we have discussed in this section lead us to the following formulation of the consumption equation:

$$(1) \quad C_t = a_0 + a_1(W_1 + W_2 - T_W)_t + a_2(P - S_P - T_P)_t +$$
$$+ a_3(A - T_A)_t + a_4 C_{t-1} + a_5(L_1)_{t-1} + a_6(N_P)_t + u_{1t}$$

C	= consumer expenditures in 1939 dollars
W_1	= deflated private employee compensation
W_2	= deflated government employee compensation
$W_1 + W_2 - T_W$	= deflated disposable employee compensation
P	= deflated nonwage nonfarm income
S_P	= deflated corporate savings
$P - S_P - T_P$	= deflated disposable nonwage nonfarm income
A	= deflated farm income
$A - T_A$	= deflated disposable farm income
L_1	= deflated end-of-year liquid assets (currency, bank deposits, saving and loan shares, and U.S. government bonds) held by persons
N_P	= number of persons in the United States
u_1	= random disturbance [1]

THE INVESTMENT EQUATION

In contrast to the preceding analysis in which we were concerned with the actions of consumers, we now turn to the behavior patterns of producers in making capital expenditures. These expenditures, gross domestic investment, in our highly aggregative model will consist of construction, purchases of producers' equipment, and the net change in inventories. This heterogeneity exceeds our ultimate desiderata, but for the particular model at hand, it will be considered acceptable.

Keynes [2]), in a volume antecedent to the presentation of the employ-

---

[1]) In each subsequent structural equation other than simple definitions, it will be understood that a disturbance is associated with the equation.

[2]) J. M. Keynes, *A Treatise on Money*, Vol. I, (London: Macmillan and Co. Ltd., 1935) p. 140.

ment theory which we so frequently cite, refers to profits as "the mainspring of change in the existing economic system." Although we are not following his precise definition of profits used on that occasion, we are attributing this key role to nonwage income in our system. Investment, one of the dynamic forces in economic activity, is, by the assumptions of our model, motivated by profit. We assume that investing as a whole is done by people who do not receive wages, although this is not strictly correct insofar as residential house purchases are included in construction.

Investment, indeed, represents change in the economic system since it is defined as the change in the stock of productive assets. Net investment, more particularly, would be measured by the change in the stock of capital, but we shall make gross investment the central concept in our equation. We feel that this corresponds more closely to behavior in which decisions are made about total capital outlays whether they be for purposes of replacement or expansion.

Keynes' investment theory contained in the notion of the *marginal efficiency of capital* equates outlays of new elements of capital to the discounted expected earning stream to be realized from the use of the physical capital in the production process. We do not have lengthy reliable series for expected earnings, but if one regarded the current and lagged earning rates as indicators of expected rates, it would be plausible to consider investment as a function of the spread between the rate of return on capital and the rate of interest,

$$\left(\frac{P+A}{K} - i\right)_t, \quad \left(\frac{P+A}{K} - i\right)_{t-1}.$$

$P + A$, measured as total nonwage income, neglecting the effect of taxes and transfers, gives essentially total property and entrepreneurial income before interest and rent charges are taken into account. In accounting terminology, it measures operating income for the total economy. The cost rate against which the rate of operating return is to be measured is the interest cost of loan funds, i. In an attempt to preserve linearity as far as possible throughout our model, we shall develop statistical equations with nonwage income, stock of capital, and interest rate as three separate linear variables. Since the overall effect of the rate of nonwage income is positive and since the stock of capital enters in the denominator of this rate, the stock variable will be expected to have a negative effect in a linearized equation. Like other asset variables included in various equations, it will be dated as of the beginning of the period for any particular stretch of time.

Since the investment variable represents gross capital outlays, we shall correspondingly make the income variable represent gross operating income by adding depreciation allowances to customary estimates of profits, rent, interest, agricultural income, etc., in the national income totals. The income variable will be placed on a disposable basis by subtracting taxes and adding transfers allocated to components of nonwage income. As mentioned in an earlier section, corporate savings will not be subtracted from income disposable for capital outlays. In this equation we shall not distinguish between different marginal propensities to invest. We combine disposable farm income and disposable nonfarm nonwage income into a single variable with a common marginal coefficient.

The appropriate interest rate to be used as a variable in the equation of investment behavior would seem to be the long term rate on private bonds. Inventory investment is the only element of our total which should be more properly related to the short term rate. In general, past statistical studies have not shown a decidedly significant effect of interest on investment. In industries where the length of life of capital goods is long, say 15–20 years at least, and where capital costs are expected to be written off gradually over that period of time, interest charges may be strategic for investment decisions. Potentially we look with favor towards a significant role of interest rates in the investment equation, but, as will become evident in the later empirical sections, we have not yet been able to make a reasonable judgment about its effect and cannot assign it a reliable nonzero value in this relation. In order to achieve a true link between the equations of the real and financial sectors of the economy, we need to find a more significant role than has yet been discovered for interest rates in the investment process. Perhaps the split at a later stage into residential construction, industrial construction, producers' equipment, and inventories will elucidate the significance of interest rates in "real" economic behavior.

The preference of many businessmen for internal as opposed to

12

external financing accounts perhaps for the dominant significance of profits compared with interest rates in the investment equation. Current and recent past profits do not, however, constitute the sole fund available for capital outlays. Liquid assets other than recent profit receipts represent a fund readily available for such purposes; therefore we introduce beginning-of-period liquid assets in the hands of enterprises as a variable in the investment equation.

Putting all these considerations together, we derive an investment equation of the form:

$$(2) \quad I_t = \beta_0 + \beta_1(P + A + D - T_P - T_A)_t + \beta_2(P + A + \\ + D - T_P - T_A)_{t-1} + \beta_3(i_L)_{t-1} + \beta_4 K_{t-1} + \beta_5(L_2)_{t-1} + u_{2t}.$$

In addition to the variables previously defined, we have

I = gross private domestic capital formation in 1939 dollars.
D = capital consumption charges in 1939 dollars.
i_L = average yield on corporate bonds.
K = end-of-year stock of private capital in 1939 dollars.
L_2 = deflated end-of-year liquid assets held by enterprises [1]).

THE CORPORATE SAVINGS EQUATION

The structural specifications in the consumption and investment equations, subtracting corporate savings from income in the former case and leaving it in income in the latter case, require us to give separate treatment to the behavior process associated with this variable.

As should be evident, corporate savings are related to corporate income. Like consumers, corporations have a propensity to save, but also like consumers it is not to be estimated from a simple linear savings function connecting total retained earnings to total income. Net corporate income after corporate taxes gives us a disposable concept needed for proper measurement of income in this equation.

Tinbergen [2]), in his equation of corporate savings behavior, used accumulated surplus as an additional variable on the assumption that

---

[1]) Holdings of farmers are included in L_1, not in L_2.
[2]) Tinbergen, *op. cit.*, p. 115.

13

internally accumulated funds would be available for dividend payment in case of inadequacy of earnings.

Dobrovolsky, [1] in a later study of corporate savings, investigated Tinbergen's hypothesis with data from a sample of manufacturing corporations covering a longer period of time, 1923–1943. He finds substantial agreement with Tinbergen's results, but on further probing discovers that lagged dividend payments are significant because of corporations' attempts to maintain a stable dividend policy. When earnings fluctuate, corporations are assumed to keep current dividends close to past dividends and let savings bear the brunt of any adjustment to the fluctuating income situation.

Our version of the corporate savings behavior equation is

$$(3) \quad (S_P)_t = \gamma_0 + \gamma_1(P_C - T_C)_t + \gamma_2(P_C - T_C - S_P)_{t-1} + \gamma_3 B_{t-1} + u_{3t}$$

P_C = deflated corporate profits.
T_C = deflated corporate income taxes.
B = deflated end-of-year corporate surplus.

THE RELATION BETWEEN CORPORATE PROFITS AND NONWAGE NONFARM INCOME

The income distinctions introduced in our consumption and investment equations distinguish among wage, farm, and nonwage nonfarm income. It is the last mentioned component which is most closely associated with corporate savings behavior; yet it includes some extraneous elements. *Corporate* income is the variable associated with *corporate* savings. As remarked previously, we do not have adequate time series statistics of total business savings, including both corporate and noncorporate flows. In addition to corporate profits, nonwage nonfarm income includes earnings of unincorporated and professional enterprise. These earnings series fluctuate rather closely with corporate earnings; so their inclusion in nonwage nonfarm income is not bothersome. It is more sluggish components like interest, rents, and royalties that make our variable P inappropriate for use in the equation of corporate savings behavior.

Since we insist upon structural estimation as far as possible within

---

[1] S. P. Dobrovolsky, *Corporate Income Retention, 1915–43*, (New York: National Bureau of Economic Research, 1951).

the confines of our aggregative system, we use P_C and not P in equation (3). This leaves us with the necessity of "explaining" P_C within a closed system. We simply put forth the empirical, nonstructural, relation for the purpose of maintaining the completeness of the model

$$(4) \qquad (P_C)_t = \delta_0 + \delta_1 P_t + \delta_2 P_{t-1} + u_{4t}.$$

By using both current and lagged values of P, we may impart some dynamic character and thereby improve this empirical relation.

The Depreciation Equation

With gross investment, I, and the stock of capital, K, appearing as separate endogenous variables in some equations of the model, it becomes necessary to treat depreciation as a separate endogenous variable because among the accounting definitions, to be enumerated later, we find that the rate of change of K is equal to $I - D$.

Depreciation data in our model are based on accounting records although they are revalued from accounting to current and constant prices. Most accounting estimates of depreciation charges are based on the straight line method applied to original cost. To clarify the meaning of this remark, let us consider a homogeneous producer good, say a machine, bought in the amount of x_t during period t. The variable x_t represents gross investment. Suppose that the machine has an estimated lifetime of h periods. At the beginning of the investment process, in period 1, we have

$$x_1 = \text{gross investment in period 1,}$$
$$\frac{1}{2h} x_1 = D_1 = \text{depreciation in period 1.}$$

During the first period the equipment depreciates by only half the usual periodic amount on the assumption that purchases are spread evenly throughout the period.

$$x_2 = \text{gross investment in period 2,}$$
$$\frac{1}{h} x_1 + \frac{1}{2h} x_2 = D_2 = \text{depreciation in period 2.}$$

The variable x_t represents money outlay during period t, and D_t represents money value of book depreciation charges during period t.

If equipment prices have changed between periods 1 and 2, one component of D_2 will be at the prices of period 1 and the other component at the prices of period 2. This is the sense in which book depreciation data are valued in accounting prices.

In general, after the investment and depreciation process has been going on for several periods, we have

$$\frac{1}{2h} x_{t-h} + \frac{1}{h} x_{t-h+1} + \ldots + \frac{1}{h} x_{t-1} + \frac{1}{2h} x_t = D_t.$$

The prices of the current period and the past h periods are averaged in determining the price level on which D_t is based.

By appropriate weighting of past prices in the durable goods sector of the economy, we can convert D_t from a measure in terms of accounting prices to a measure in terms of current or constant prices. In constant prices, depreciation is a moving average of past values of gross investment measured also in constant prices. The length of the moving average is determined by the average lifetime of capital goods.

In our model we have used estimates of depreciation revalued to constant prices but do not have explicit series of gross investment prior to 1929; therefore, we did not assume depreciation to be strictly a moving average of past gross investment. Instead, we let depreciation depend on the size of the stock of capital. This gives an approximation to the mechanical aspect of depreciation, the amount of capital consumption that goes on regardless of the rate of utilization. The level of aggregate economic activity, showing the degree of utilization of capital, may also be important in inducing entrepreneurs to depart from conventional straight line methods. Our depreciation equation thus takes the form

(5) $\quad D_t = \varepsilon_0 + \varepsilon_1 \dfrac{K_t + K_{t-1}}{2} + \varepsilon_3(Y + T + D - W_2)_t + u_{5t}.$

$Y + T + D - W_2 =$ private gross national product in 1939 dollars.

The Demand for Labor Equation

It is well known that profit maximization under conditions of exponential production functions [1] implies constant factor shares,

---

[1] These are functions of the general Cobb-Douglas variety, linear in the logarithms of inputs and outputs.

with each factor's constant being its production elasticity. Thus relations expressing the constancy of labor's share of total output can be interpreted as variations of marginal productivity or labor demand equations.

We have relaxed the strict conditions and implications for such relations but retain their general form. In our linear model we shall find it convenient not to assume absolute proportionality between the wage bill and the value of output. We shall allow the wage bill to depend in a more general linear fashion on both current and lagged values of output. We shall also permit a smooth trend to modify this relation. The profit maximization interpretation of the equation applies only to private employment. We use the private wage bill and the value of private production as variables in this equation.

$$(6) \quad (W_1)_t = \zeta_0 + \zeta_1(Y + T + D - W_2)_t + \zeta_2(Y + T + D - W_2)_{t-1} + \zeta_3 t + u_{6t}.$$

t = time trend in years.

THE PRODUCTION FUNCTION

A feature of the present model is less condensation than previously of the supply side of the market. In our attempt to lay bare a process of absolute wage and price determination we shall also have use for the equation of the productive process.

In the aggregative economy, raw materials cancel out, and land is effectively held constant. In production studies of sectors of the economy, many specific inputs must be considered, but these are not relevant in our grossly aggregative function. Moreover, in an economy less self sufficient than the United States, imports of raw materials and producers' equipment must be regarded as factors of production. Our production function, however, will contain only labor and capital as inputs. We shall also allow for gradual technological change with a time trend.

The appropriate labor input variable for the production function is a measure of man hours, although many aggregative studies in this country have used the number of men as an input measure. We have multiplied estimates of the number of workers by an index of hours

17

worked per year. To this corrected measure of men, we have added the number of entrepreneurs and farmers. We assume that members of the latter two groups always work a full period of time. Our production equation is

$$(7) \quad (Y + T + D - W_2)_t = \eta_0 + \eta_1[h(N_W - N_G) + N_E + N_F]_t +$$

$$+ \eta_2 \frac{K_t + K_{t-1}}{2} + \eta_3 t + u_{7t}.$$

h = index of hours worked per person per year.
N_W = number of wage – and salary – earners.
N_G = number of government employees.
N_E = number of nonfarm entrepreneurs.
N_F = number of farm operators.

THE LABOR MARKET ADJUSTMENT EQUATION

The strategic equation for determining the level of absolute wages and prices in the system; in fact the only equation, thus far, that is not written in terms of "real" or deflated variables; is our equation to show wage bargaining in the labor market. Without claiming that workers are blinded by "money illusion," we merely build into this equation the institutional observation that wage negotiations are usually in terms of money and not real wages. We do not rule out the possibility that workers bargain for money wage increases because prices have increased. It is precisely the well known wage-price lag that makes this equation nonhomogeneous in money variables. The lag is shortened by "escalator clauses" in wage contracts, but it persists. We have not used data for shorter periods than one year, and consequently have a rather long wage-price lag, but in shorter run models it would be possible to reduce the length of lag.

The main reasoning behind this equation is that of the law of supply and demand. Money wage rates move in response to excess supply or excess demand on the labor market. High unemployment represents high excess supply, and low unemployment below customary frictional levels represents excess demand.

We have lived in an age of general inflation; hence, money wage rates show a general upward trend. The entire relation is

18

$$(8) \quad w_t - w_{t-1} = \theta_0 + \theta_1(N - N_W - N_E - N_F)_t +$$
$$+ \theta_2(p_{t-1} - p_{t-2}) + \theta_3 t + u_{8t}.$$

w	$=$ index of hourly wages.
N	$=$ number of persons in the labor force.
$N - N_W - N_E - N_F$	$=$ unemployment in number of persons.
p	$=$ general price index.

The Import Demand Equation

It is frequently said that foreign trade is unimportant for the United States. It is true that the net foreign balance is a small component of total national product, but obviously neither total exports nor total imports are nearly as small as the net balance. In some econometric studies, the net foreign balance is conveniently assumed to be purely an exogenous variable dependent on the politics of external affairs of the United States.

Imports are surely not exogenous; they are closely tied to economic activity in this country. We shall treat them in our model in much the same way as other commodities and services demanded by domestic consumers and producers.

A principal determinant of import demand is domestic disposable income. Finished products imported are sold directly, after passing through transitory channels, to consumers. Raw materials, for the most part, are manufactured into finished consumer goods. Consequently, the role of disposable income is not surprising.

Relative prices between foreign and domestic products would also seem to be relevant in this equation. Statistical studies of aggregate imports have been inconclusive on the effects of relative prices, perhaps because of their intercorrelation with income and the dominant importance of the latter variable. It is in this area that we anticipate improved results from a less aggregative model with imports subdivided into finer classes.

If we deflate money income in the import equation by the price of imports, and have income deflated by the general price level as a variable in other equations of the system, we can implicitly take account of both income and relative price effects in a single term in our equation. The simple algebra of this device which avoids the problem of intercorrelation can be seen in the import equation below. In this equation we also have lagged imports to show the effect of the past in the same way as was done in the consumption function.

$$(9) \quad (F_I)_t = \iota_0 + \iota_1\left[(W_1 + W_2 + P + A - T_W - T_P - T_A)\frac{p}{p_I}\right]_t +$$
$$+ \iota_2(F_I)_{t-1} + u_{9t}.$$

F_I = imports of goods and services in 1939 dollars.

p_I = index of prices of imports.

$W_1 + W_2 + P + A - T_W - T_P - T_A$ = deflated disposable income plus corporate savings.

The bracketed expression in (9) is thus a measure of disposable income deflated by an index of import prices.

The Agricultural Income Determination Equation

On the demand side of the market, we have had occasion to single out the behavior of farmers because they have a high propensity to save (average and marginal). We must now consider agriculture as a producing sector in order that our system be closed in the endogenous variables, among which is agricultural income.

There are numerous reasons for going into great detail in explaining agricultural production and supply. Just as farmers are unique in their consumer demand patterns so is agricultural output unique in that it is a type of commodity with extremely inelastic supply. Climatic and other crop conditions are of dominant importance in determining available quantities. Economic forces, particularly those operative in the short run, are relatively uninfluential.

We shall, however, reserve to later study a detailed model of agricultural production. A comparatively inexpensive solution to our present problem will be the following: Suppose we have a large system of equations, say n, in a large number of variables, say $n + m$, describing all the structural relations of the agricultural sector. Of these variables, n are internal to the agricultural sector, and m are external. By successive substitution this $n \times (n + m)$ system can be reduced to a $1 \times (1 + m)$ system in which one endogenous agricultural variable is a function of m variables outside agriculture. An equation derived in this way by successive substitution will lack autonomy, but it is as close to being a structural relation as our resources permit at this stage of the research effort.

A major variable influencing agricultural demand, and therefore one of the external variables in the full equation system of the sector, is income outside agriculture. Another external demand variable is foreign demand. We shall use an index of agricultural exports to show foreign demand. One of the most important external supply variables would be an indicator of weather conditions. In studying agriculture for the whole economy, it is difficult and seemingly impossible to devise an overall weather index that would be a useful variable in explaining the production of cotton, tobacco, spring wheat, winter wheat, corn, hogs, beef, lamb, fruits, vegetables, etc. simultaneously. Growing seasons, plant physiology, and geography are so diverse over the whole country that we have not used a climatic variable in the single reduced equation although in a slightly disaggregated model it may prove to be feasible.

An extremely important exogenous factor in both agricultural supply and demand is government price support policy. This policy is designed to keep prices received by farmers from falling relative to prices paid. Official indexes of prices paid and received are used by law, but as indexes of agriculture's terms of trade in our model, we use the ratio between an index of prices received by farmers and the general price index for the whole economy. In addition to outright subsidies to agriculture under other programs, the price support policy has operated through a system of production loans to farmers which they need not repay in the face of unfavorable prices. This amounts to a subsidy in fact. In some years, however, redemptions of these loans by farmers may exceed the amount taken out and thereby give rise to a negative component of agricultural income.

The terms of trade for agriculture have divergent effects on farm income. Unfavorable terms may stimulate demand by persons outside agriculture, but it requires an elasticity of demand larger than unity for a drop in prices to increase income, and most farm products are suspected of having inelastic demand. [1]) Unfavorable terms of trade

---

[1]) See Karl A. Fox, "Factors Affecting Farm Income, Farm Prices, and Food Consumption," *Agricultural Economics Research*, U.S. Department of Agriculture. Vol. III, pp. 65–82, esp. Tables 6 and 7, pp. 76–77.

call forth government subsidy to maintain agricultural income. They also discourage supply, although only with some lag. In an equation with agricultural income a function of the terms of trade we cannot be certain of the direction of the net marginal effect on a priori grounds. As in the import equation we shall use the price index of agricultural products to deflate nonagricultural income and thus introduce the terms of trade as a multiplier of income deflated by the general price index.

Our equation for agricultural income is

$$(10) \quad \left(A\frac{p}{p_A}\right)_t = \varkappa_0 + \varkappa_1\left[(W_1 + W_2 + P - S_P - T_W - T_P)\frac{p}{p_A}\right]_t +$$
$$+ \varkappa_2\left[(W_1 + W_2 + P - S_P - T_W - T_P)\frac{p}{p_A}\right]_{t-1} +$$
$$+ \varkappa_3\left(\frac{p}{p_A}\right)_t + \varkappa_4(F_A)_t + u_{10,t}.$$

p_A = index of agricultural prices.
F_A = index of agricultural exports.
$W_1 + W_2 + P - S_P - T_W - T_P$ = deflated disposable nonfarm income.

THE RELATION BETWEEN AGRICULTURAL AND NONAGRICULTURAL PRICES

Insofar as the government is successful in its price support policy, there will tend to be a relationship between agricultural and non-agricultural prices. A scatter diagram of these two price indexes shows a remarkable degree of relationship.

A simple linear relation between these two prices does not bring out all the intricacies of the laws of price support; however, those laws are too complicated to be expressed directly in our model.

Price supports do not work perfectly, and they provide floors without ceilings to farm prices. There is some element of market influence on agricultural price movements. In more detailed models with inventory holding and price speculation, it is often possible to derive autoregressive equations of price fluctuations. [1]) In addition

---

[1]) See A. Kisselgoff, *Factors Affecting the Demand for Consumer Instalment Sales Credit*, (New York: National Bureau of Economic Research, Technical Paper 7, 1952), pp. 22–23.

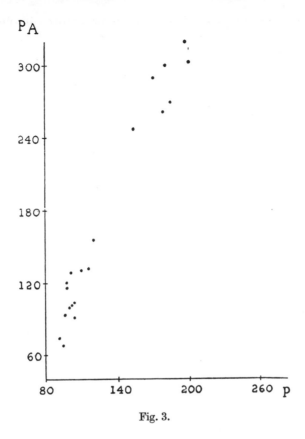

Fig. 3.

to the relation to nonagricultural prices, we may have agricultural prices depend on their own lagged values.

$$(11) \qquad (p_A)_t = \lambda_0 + \lambda_1 p_t + \lambda_2 (p_A)_{t-1} + u_{11,t}.$$

The Household Liquidity Preference Equation

In our model, we have already introduced two liquidity variables, household and business holdings of liquid assets. Although both these variables are lagged in equations (1) and (2) because they are treated as *initial conditions* in consumption and investment planning over time, they are still endogenous variables from an economic point of view. In our model, there is a difference between the statistical and

23

economic treatment of these variables. Since they are purely lagged in the equations discussed thus far, they might, from a statistical viewpoint, be treated like other predetermined variables, say the truly exogenous factors. But then the model would then be lacking in a full explanation of economic fluctuations. If we want to use the model to obtain a complete picture of cyclical characteristics, we cannot dispense with liquidity preference equations. Another way of putting this more formally is to note that we cannot derive final equations which are autoregressive in the endogenous variables and dependent on purely exogenous variables unless the estimated liquidity preference equations or substitutes for them are included in the model.

For households, we assume that the main choices are between holding securities or cash. They cannot hold an appreciable amount in the form of goods other than houses and some durables. The function of a liquidity preference equation at the household level is to show how consumers decide how much cash and what value of securities to hold. Consumers do not hold appreciable amounts of short term securities. They hold either long term bonds or stocks. We are not including share prices of equities in our model and hence take the long term interest rate to be indicative of the return to consumers for parting with money and investing in securities.

The classical economic theory of cash holding assumes total cash balances to be held in proportion to income. The factor of proportionality is a basic parameter in the classical system. Keynes, in his *General Theory*, claimed that all cash was not transactions cash, part of it being speculative and precautionary holdings. The ratio of cash to income is a variable, not a parameter, in the Keynesian system. This variable depends on interest and possibly the level of income. A general trivariate relation among money, interest rate, and income can be assumed.

Keynes, however, gave some specifications about the form of the liquidity preference function. He recognized the existence of transactions balances proportional to income and assumed the remainder of balances to be a function of the interest rate alone. Instead of viewing money as a general joint function of two variables, he considered it to be composed of two additive functions, each one separately dependent on a single variable. While he retained the nature of the classical transactions formula — proportionality between balances and income — he assumed that the speculative portion depending on interest rates should have infinite elasticity at low rates. The minimum rate needed to cover the costs of financial services provided an asymptote. This may be in the neighborhood of one or two percent.

In empirical studies following Keynes' theory, a statistical device was adopted for separating balances into two parts, transactions and idle balances. [1]) During some historical period of high turnover of cash and high level economic activity, the ratio between cash balances and income is calculated. This ratio is assumed to be an estimate of the classical parameter on the assumption that no balances are idle during this period of brisk turnover and brisk trade. In other periods, any balances held in excess of this estimated fraction of income are assumed to be idle balances.

Let $M_t =$ deflated personal holdings of currency and checking accounts at the end of year t.

$(W_1 + W_2 + P + A - T_W - T_P - S_P - T_A)_t =$ deflated disposable income during year t.

We calculate the ratio

$$\frac{M_t}{(W_1 + W_2 + P + A - T_W - T_P - S_P - T_A)_t}$$

for a series of years and find

$$\frac{M_{1929}}{(W_1 + W_2 + P + A - T_W - T_P - S_P - T_A)_{1929}} = 0.14.$$

This is the smallest value of the ratio in our sample period. [2]) The ratio is the inverse of a velocity measure; therefore, we have maximum transactions velocity and brisk trade in 1929. We assume this year to be one in which currency and checking accounts were not idle. For other years we measure idle balances as

$$(L_1)_t - 0.14(W_1 + W_2 + P + A - T_W - T_P - S_P - T_A)_t.$$

[1]) J. Tobin, "Liquidity Preference and Monetary Policy," *The Review of Economics and Statistics,* Vol. XXIX, 1947, pp. 124–31. See also A. J. Brown, "Interest, Prices and the Demand Schedule for Idle Money," *Oxford Economic Papers,* No. 2, 1939, pp. 46–69.

[2]) It would also be the smallest if the beginning of the period were considerably earlier than 1929, the first year in our sample.

In L_1 we include savings deposits, U.S. government bonds, savings and loan shares, as well as demand deposits and currency. The additional items are, by their very nature, assumed to be idle balances. The relationship between idle balances, so calculated, and the long term interest rate can be seen from the accompanying chart.

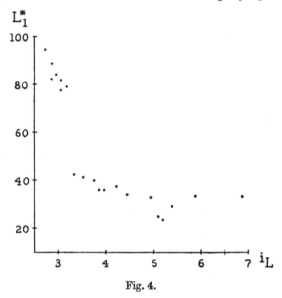

Fig. 4.

The general shape follows that suggested by the Keynesian hypotheses. We represent this equation by the expression

$$(12) \quad (L_1)_t - \mu_1(W_1 + W_2 + P + A - T_W - T_P - S_P - T_A)_t = \\ = \mu_0[(i_L)_t - i_L^0]^{\mu_2} u_{12,t}.$$

i_L = average yield on corporate bonds in percent.

i_L^0 = minimum possible interest rate.

A mathematical function with the shape given in (12) fits well to the scatter of points in Figure 4. The parameters μ_1 and i_L^0 are fixed in advance of estimation of μ_0 and μ_2. The left hand side of (12) measures idle balances, the ordinate in Figure 4.

THE BUSINESS LIQUIDITY PREFERENCE EQUATION

The motivation behind business holding of cash balances is undoubt-

26

edly different from that of individuals because the choices are not made among the same possibilities. Businesses do hold large stocks of commodities in the form of inventories; thus we shall assume them to be making three-way choices among money, securities, and goods. Moreover, the major business choice between securities and goods is a short-run decision, whether to hold inventories for a short period or to hold short-term securities (commercial paper); whether to borrow for a short period or to forego the possibility of inventory gains.

The cost of short-run borrowing, or the return to the holder of short term securities, is measured by the short-term rate of interest, a rate to be distinguished from the long-term rate used in the investment and household liquidity preference equations. This is another example of economic specification contributing to the identification of structural relationships in our model.

The unit gain on inventories is a capital gain measured by the price appreciation during the time of holding. Similarly a price depreciation brings about capital losses except in the case of "short selling." Two interesting behavioral aspects are brought out by this consideration. In the first place, inventory gains or losses occur only if a change takes place. Prices must move up or down. In contrast, income on securities can be realized at the current rate of interest without any change occurring. Secondly, nonhomogeneity in prices is assumed. There must be changes in the absolute level of prices in order that gains or losses be realized on the whole of inventories. [1]) It is generally true that speculation is associated with dynamic relations that do not follow the traditional homogeneity postulate of classical equilibrium economics.

Business firms have the same transactions motive as households. For reasons of convenience they must have spendable cash on hand to meet current transactions. In particular we assume that business holdings for transactions purposes are proportional to current business costs. These costs are mainly for wages and materials. Materials cancel in the system as a whole, disregarding imports; therefore, in our aggregative model we have business holdings for transactions purposes

---

[1]) Relative price changes with a constant absolute price index would permit gains or losses on particular types of inventories.

proportional to the wage bill. As in the previous equation for households, we could estimate transactions balances by calculating the minimal ratio of currency and demand deposits to the wage bill and subtracting this ratio times the current wage bill from current liquid assets of each time period considered. [1])

In our multivariate equation with the rate of change in prices present as well as the level of short term interest rates, we have not specified any particular nonlinear function like the infinite elasticity of personal liquidity preferences at low interest rates. We have also modified our linear function of business holdings of liquid assets by introducing an inertia effect which states that firms tend to hold the same balances as in the previous period except for modifications brought about by the level of the wage bill, the rate of change of prices, or the level of the short-term interest rate. Our full equation is

$$(13) \quad (L_2)_t - \nu_1(W_1)_t = \nu_0 + \nu_2(p_t - p_{t-1}) + \nu_3(i_S)_t + \nu_4(L_2)_{t-1} + u_{13,t}.$$

i_S = average yield on short term commercial paper.

The Relation between Short and Long Term Interest Rates

The interest rate structure is a complicated matter, and in the future we expect to give more explicit attention to its details for a more disaggregated model. In present circumstances we merely try to tie our two rates together by an approach which stems from a definition and some empirical estimation.

It is commonly stated that the long term rate of interest is a moving average of expected short term rates. [2]) Short term rates fluctuate relatively more than long term rates; therefore investors in forming an expected value of future short term rates may take into account a complex pattern of recently observed short rates. We have experimented with various linear combinations of lagged values in an effort to deduce an empirical time series expression for expected short

---

[1]) For an application of this approach to a sample of corporations see A. Kisselgoff, "Liquidity Preference of Large Manufacturing Corporations, (1921–1939)," *Econometrica*, Vol. 13, 1945, pp. 334–344.

[2]) See e.g. David Durand, *Basic Yields of Corporate Bonds, 1900–1942*, (New York: National Bureau of Economic Research, Technical Paper No. 3, 1942), pp. 18–19.

term rates. Our equation, based to a large extent on empirical manipulation, is [1])

(14) $$(i_L)_t = \xi_0 + \xi_1(i_S)_{t-3} + \xi_2(i_S)_{t-5} + u_{14,t}.$$

The reader should not adopt the mistaken view that we have transposed the traditional lead-lag relation between long and short rates. *Expected future short rates are related to current long rates.* This does not necessarily imply that actual short rates are a function of past long rates. Our equation measures expected future short rates by the proxy expression

$$\xi_1(i_S)_{t-3} + \xi_2(i_S)_{t-5}$$

pression, but our justification for this is purely empirical and not structural.

THE MONEY MARKET ADJUSTMENT EQUATION

We used a version of the fundamental "law of supply and demand" to show how absolute wages or prices are determined in our model. The rate of change of money wage rates, in equation (8), is made a function of unemployment, a measure of excess labor supply, and other variables.

The analogous relation in the money market is between excess reserves and the rate of change of interest rates. With large excess reserves, banks can readily lend and would be pushed towards lowering interest rates in order to dispose of their excesses. With a tight money market and deposits close to the legal limit, there would be a tendency towards raising interest rates. We have introduced a scaling factor in this relation. Instead of using total excess reserves, we have used as our measure of excess supply the percentage of total reserves in excess of requirements. This measure is probably more accurately determined than total excess reserves because the number of reporting banks varies over the time period covered. Since we have reports for most banks including virtually all of the large banks, the percentage of reserves held in excess should be given quite accurately as an estimate for the entire banking system. Correspondingly we have not used the absolute change in interest rates, but the percentage change as for our other variable. The short term rate was selected as that which responds, in the first instance, to the condition of bank reserves.

---

[1]) Compare with the equation connecting long and short rates in M. Kalecki, "The Short-term and the Long-term Rate of Interest," *Studies in Economic Dynamics*, (London: George Allen and Unwin, Ltd., 1943).

This would be reasonable if the major use of bank reserves were for short term loans to business.

During recent years, the Federal Reserve Board supported the level of bond prices by coming into the market to buy government securities whenever they showed signs of selling below par. Under these conditions one would be tempted to redefine excess reserves to include bank holdings of government securities, for these are as good as cash to holders as long as there is government price support. Empirically we found no reasonable relationship between the rate of change of interest rates and excess reserves defined to include government security holdings by banks. This is in contrast to the relation we observe between the rate of change of interest rates and a conventional measure of excess reserves. The relation, in any case, is relatively weak and possibly calls for more intensive research. The scatter plots of the two relations are given in Figures 5 and 6.

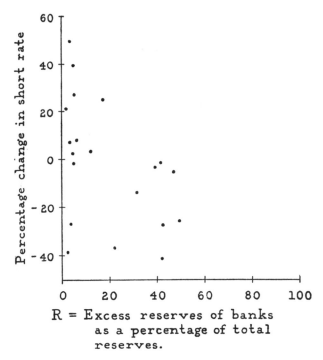

R = Excess reserves of banks
as a percentage of total
reserves.

Fig. 5.

30

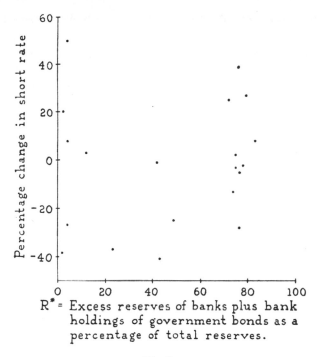

Fig. 6.

We have based our money market adjustment equation on the relation found in figure 5. Symbolically it is

$$(15) \qquad \frac{(i_S)_t - (i_S)_{t-1}}{(i_S)_{t-1}} = o_0 + o_1 R_t + u_{15,t}.$$

Definitions and Accounting Identities

Because of notational simplification and convention, we have chosen to write our system in a particular form which uses more variables than necessary. Some of these variables are tied together by definitions or identities. The double entry nature of an accounting system is responsible for some of these.

In econometric models, the various accounting equations have been treated as pure identities, equations that must hold for all time periods for whatever values the variables assume in that time period. But as every national income statistician knows, this is not always simple to achieve. We have forced this requirement, however, in the present model by measuring key variables in such a way as to fulfill all definitions precisely.

The components of gross national product are used at various places throughout the model. In some equations we deal with consumer expenditures, in others with capital formation, and in others with imports. Combining these variables appropriately with some exogenous variables, we have the definition of gross national product as

$$(16) \qquad C_t + I_t + G_t + (F_E)_t - (F_I)_t = Y_t + T_t + D_t.$$

New exogenous variables not previously defined are

G = government expenditures for goods and services in 1939 dollars.

F_E = exports of goods and services in 1939 dollars.

T = deflated indirect taxes less subsidies.

Wherever we used the variable $Y + T + D$ in the model, we could equally well have replaced it by the left hand side of (16). This would have kept the number of endogenous variables smaller by eliminating Y. At the same time we would drop equation (16). Thus we see that this definitional equation plays no role in the model other than serving to keep our thinking well organized.

Conceptually, we know that we must come to the same total for national production or income whether we reckon in terms of expenditure flows or income flows. This remark assumes that appropriate and well known allowances have been made for indirect taxes and subsidies, items used to bridge the gap between market prices and factor costs in national income accounting. *Independent* measurements of national income and of national product are not necessarily identical except for the above bridging items. This is true because of measurement error involved in assigning values to the various components of income and expenditure flows. The irreconcilable residual is known as the statistical discrepancy. In our model we have not chosen purely independent measures of both the income and expenditure sides of the national accounts; therefore, we also make use of the identity [1])

$$(17) \qquad (W_1)_t + (W_2)_t + P_t + A_t = Y_t.$$

[1]) In our model, the statistical discrepancy is, in fact, imbedded in our variable T

These variables, which have been previously defined, comprise the national income. If we were to make our best estimate of each item in equations (16) and (17), we may find, on putting them together, that we have, not an identity, but the stochastic equation

$$C_t + I_t + G_t + (F_E)_t - (F_I)_t = (W_1)_t + (W_2)_t + P_t + A_t + D_t + T_t + u_{16,t}.$$

The error, $u_{16,t}$, arises because of observational inaccuracy, and under many circumstances may be regarded as a random variable like $u_{1t}, u_{2t}, \ldots, u_{15,t}$. The only difference between $u_{16,t}$ and the others is that the former can be observed. This happens because the stochastic equation in which $u_{16,t}$ occurs has all known coefficients (either plus or minus unity). In contrast, the other stochastic equations of the model have unknown parameters.

Another identity in the system connects the wage rate, hours of work, employment and the wage bill. We have used all these variables separately in some equations of the model, but they are tied together by the relation

(18) $$h_t \frac{w_t}{p_t} (N_W)_t = (W_1)_t + (W_2)_t.$$

One variable is measured as a residual, after all others have been independently measured. This insures fulfillment of (18).

It was remarked earlier, in connection with the investment equation, that investment can be considered to be the rate of change in the stock of capital. Capital has been measured by cumulating the net investment of each period to initial values; hence, we append the definition

(19) $$K_t - K_{t-1} = I_t - D_t.$$

In the same way corporate surplus was defined as the accumulation of net corporate savings. The analogous equation is

(20) $$B_t - B_{t-1} = (S_P)_t.$$

III. SOME PROPERTIES OF THE SYSTEM

In the preceding section, each equation of the model was discussed as it was introduced. The properties of each equation considered by itself occupied our central attention there. We shall now consider more of the properties of the model viewed as a system.

One of the most important distinctions contained in this structural system is that between endogenous and exogenous variables. It is not possible to understand the economic mechanism involved nor indeed to estimate the parameters without a clear distinction between these two types of variables. In a general way we may say that the exogenous variables together with initial conditions and disturbances move the closed system of endogenous variables through time.

The endogenous variables are:

p = price index of gross national product (1939 base: 100).
C = consumer expenditures in 1939 dollars.
W_1 = deflated private employee compensation.
P = deflated nonwage nonfarm income.
S_P = deflated corporate savings.
A = deflated farm income.
L_1 = deflated end-of-year liquid assets held by persons.
I = gross private domestic capital formation in 1939 dollars.
D = capital consumption charges in 1939 dollars.
i_L = average yield on corporate bonds.
K = end-of-year stock of private capital in 1939 dollars.
L_2 = deflated end-of-year liquid assets held by enterprises.
P_C = deflated corporate profits.
B = deflated end-of-year corporate surplus.
Y = deflated national income.
N_W = number of wage – and salary – earners.
w = index of hourly wages (1939 base: 122.1).
F_I = imports of goods and services in 1939 dollars.

p_A = index of agricultural prices (1939 base: 100).
i_S = average yield on short term commercial paper.

These number twenty in quantity; thus the system is constructed to have equality between the number of equations and endogenous variables. These variables are traditional economic magnitudes referring in some part, at least, to activities in the private sectors of the system.

It is always easy to justify the designation of a variable as endogenous although it may have the consequence of forcing theory construction overambitiously. As much as possible, we are pushing present research to expand the scope of endogenous magnitudes. A purist's definition of exogenous variables (those that influence the system without being influenced by the system) would leave relatively little in this category. Variables resulting from natural forces such as climate and weather are perhaps the only cases of pure exogenous factors.

Our general procedure is to classify variables from the public sector in the exogenous category. We assume these to be the result of non-economic political decisions. Similarly variables determined largely by forces outside the United States are assumed to be exogenous to our single country model. Characteristics of the labor force are also assumed to be exogenous because they are heavily influenced by demographic trends. This assumption is probably the least tenable and should be one of the first to be dropped in future research. [1]

The exogenous variables are

W_2 = deflated government employee compensation.
T_W = deflated personal and payroll taxes less transfers associated with wage and salary income.
T_P = deflated personal and corporate taxes less transfers associated with nonwage nonfarm income.
T_A = deflated taxes less transfers associated with farm income.
N_P = number of persons in the United States.

---

[1] In an econometric model of long run trends in the United States since 187ᴼ, S. Vail of the Research Seminar in Quantitative Economics of the University of Michigan has treated population growth as an endogenous variable dependent upon the productivity of the economic system and its ability to provide goods for an expanding population.

T_C = deflated corporate income taxes.

t = time trend in years.

h = index of hours worked per person per year (1939 base: 1.00).

N_G = number of government employees.

N_E = number of nonfarm entrepreneurs.

N_F = number of farm operators.

N = number of persons in the labor force.

p_I = index of prices of imports (1939 base: 100).

F_A = index of agricultural exports (1939 base: 100).

R = excess reserves of banks as a percentage of total reserves.

G = government expenditures for goods and services in 1939 dollars.

F_E = exports of goods and services in 1939 dollars.

T = deflated indirect taxes less subsidies.

Two aspects of government controlled variables deserve further comment. The assumption made here is that "real" or deflated magnitudes are directly controlled. Government budgeting is actually done in current dollar units. Legislators are assumed to take current market conditions into account and correspondingly appropriate dollar amounts that will just command the real resources they desire. For statistical convenience, we have assumed this type of behavior in past observations; however, in *forecasting* we have followed the more realistic procedure of assuming only current dollar magnitudes to be exogenous. This has its complications even at this stage of analysis. For estimation from past samples we have sacrificed a certain amount of internal consistency in return for simplifying advantages.

A similar problem occurs in connection with tax collections or transfer payments. Legislators do not fix total collections or payments by law; they fix *rates*. To an even greater extent than in problems of compensating appropriations for price and wage movements, legislators attempt to set rates at levels that will secure a given flow of collections or payments. In popular renditions of tax legislation, we usually read of the effect of changes in laws on the dollar value of total collections. These magnitudes are purely estimates of the returns resulting from given rates at an assumed income level. Often we find these estimates in error, although we do recognize a very conscious effort to set rates in order to obtain preassigned collections. For purposes of estimation from past data, we regard total collections and payments (deflated) as exogenous, but in forecasting we shall be more realistic and assume only that rates are given.

The forecasting problem has its inherent interest in connection with the present model because of some basic nonlinearities involved. The nonlinearities are termed basic because they are part of our economic theory of price determination. In some cases, where we deem it appropriate, we follow conventional or classical principles and make our equations "real." They are linear relations connecting constant dollar magnitudes, deflated magnitudes, *relative* prices, or physical variables without monetary dimensions. In a system built wholly with such variables we would not be able to determine the absolute price level if we deny the validity of the classical money equation, as indeed we must,

$$\frac{M}{p} = kY.$$

In this version we have the total deflated value of cash balances proportional to the deflated value of income. This equation is linear in deflated quantities. If we had a linear model associating price ratios, real quantities, deflated values, and physical variables together with this classical equation of exchange, it would not be difficult to derive forecasting equations.

Our model has somewhat different properties. It does not have the classical money equation. It also permits departures from homogeneity conditions and uses, strategically, absolute prices or wages in certain equations instead of relative prices or wages. Speculation and market bargaining are important phenomena calling for the use of absolute prices and wages. If we were to treat inventories separately in our model, as we eventually must do, there will be even more equations with dynamic speculative elements calling for the use of absolute prices.

Since in some places we have relative prices and in others absolute prices, the system viewed as a unit is not linear. The end result of algebraic substitution and elimination brings us to polynomials for the final equation which expresses some unlagged endogenous variable as a function of predetermined variables alone.

First, let us consider the example of forecasting for one year in which deflated values of government variables T, T_W, G, etc. are considered known and predetermined. In the consumption equation (1), we assign values to $(W_2)_t$, $(T_W)_t$, $(T_P)_t$, $(T_A)_t$, C_{t-1}, $(L_1)_{t-1}$ and $(N_P)_t$. This gives us a linear relation between C_t, $(W_1)_t$, P_t, $(S_P)_t$, and A_t. Similarly values are assigned to known variables in each of the other equations.

The liquidity preference equations are responsible for two types of nonlinearity. The demand for household balances is an exponential function, while the demand for business balances depends on the absolute price level. Since we have found empirically, as will be seen later, that the interest rate plays no role, or, at best, a very uncertain or weak role in the investment equation, the monetary equations split from the rest of the system for purposes of forecasting. The result is that the system can be reduced by algebraic manipulation to a cubic equation in p_t, provided values are assigned to all predetermined variables for the forecast period, t.

If instead of assigning predetermined values to such variables as T_t, G_t, $(T_W)_t$ and others in the model, we adopt the somewhat more realistic procedure of assuming that public authorities fix only current dollar values and tax rates, we proceed differently and derive a more complicated final equation. In place of using a fixed value for G_t derived from a priori inspection of public budgets, we use, on the basis of the same documents,

$G_t^* = p_t G_t =$ current dollar government expenditures on goods and services

as the predetermined variable. A refinement may be introduced by using a specific price deflator for government expenditures, different from p_t. We would then have to assume a simple relation between this deflator and the general price level, p_t, in order to maintain the completeness of the system. By inserting the variable $\dfrac{G_t^*}{p_t}$ into the equations of the system with an assigned value for G_t^*, we increase the degree of nonlinearity in the final forecast solution since p_t occurs in the denominator of this variable.

An approximation to tax collections out of, and transfer payments into, wage income would be given by

$$(T_W)_t = a + b(W_1 + W_2)_t.$$

38

The parameters, a and b, in this equation must be estimated. If tax laws were much simpler than they, in fact, are, we could determine the parameters directly from the legal definitions. However, with exemptions, deductions, differential rates, progressivity, etc., the relationship is actually very complicated and not expressible precisely in terms of two parameters in a linear equation.

In the early forecasts prepared for postwar planning, the practice was to assume a probable tax structure for the prediction period and estimate, item by item, the amounts of taxes and transfers associated with each of a few selected income levels. A smooth relation, usually a straight line, was fitted to these *hypothetical* points, and its parameters were the unknown coefficients in the equation above. If we are now forecasting for a period in which the tax laws are to be the same as those prevailing in the past few periods (years or quarters), direct observations can be made on $(T_W)_t$, $(W_1 + W_2)_t$ and corresponding variables in similar tax-transfer-income equations. A straight line fitted to two or three observed points gives us estimates of a and b. If the tax laws are to be different in the forecast period from the preceding two or three periods, we must make some adjustments. We can often single out components for which the laws are going to change and determine the effect on the parameters for a given alteration in these components. For example, if legislation is introduced to cut personal income tax rates by 10 percent at all income levels, we can add up for each past observation period all the components of T_W except personal income taxes. Ninety percent of this component is added to the other components and the total is plotted against $(W_1 + W_2)_t$ for each of the two or three past observation periods. These data are then used to estimate a and b, the unknown parameters.

In principle, it should be possible to estimate an equation of the form

$$(T_W)_t = a_t + b_t(W_1 + W_2)_t$$

for each sample period on the basis of legal structure and observable data. These relations with known parameters could then be used as restrictions together with the structural equations in estimating the other equations of the model. As stated previously we do not use this approach. We assume $(T_W)_t$ to be an exogenous variable for the sample observations.

Since $(T_W)_t$ and $(W_1 + W_2)_t$ are both deflated values, we cannot interpret them directly in association with laws about taxes and transfers, for these latter regulations are written in terms of current dollar magnitudes. Denoting current dollar magnitudes by an asterisk, we actually estimate from recent past data, the relation

$$(T_W^*)_t = a + b(W_1^* + W_2^*)_t.$$

For the forecast period, we use in the model

$$\frac{(T_W^*)_t}{p_t} = \frac{a}{p_t} + b\,\frac{(W_1^* + W_2^*)_t}{p_t}$$

or

$$(T_W)_t = \frac{a}{p_t} + b(W_1 + W_2)_t.$$

Because of the term a/p_t, which is usually of some significance, we increase the degree of nonlinearity in the system. The same procedure is followed for the treatment of T_P, T_A, T_C, and T in forecasting. As a result the final equations for the estimation of p and Y in the forecast period take the form

$$Y_t(a_0 + a_1 p_t) + a_2 + a_3\,\frac{1}{p_t} + a_4 p_t = 0,$$

$$\frac{1}{p_t}\left(b_0 + b_1\,\frac{1}{p_t} + b_2 Y_t\right)\left(b_3 + b_4\,\frac{1}{p_t} + b_5 Y_t\right) + b_6 + b_7\,\frac{1}{p_t} + b_8 Y_t = 0,$$

where the a's and b's are combinations of structural parameters and predetermined variables. Simple "cut-and-try" methods progress rapidly towards a solution; i.e. values of p and Y which simultaneously satisfy the two nonlinear equations. Since we know the neighborhood of the solution in advance, it is not difficult to find a solution to the desired degree of approximation quickly.

These particular nonlinear forecasting equations are deduced from our model assuming that the money market equations split from the others in a particular way. The long term interest rate, an endogenous variable, appears tentatively in the investment equation and again in the equations of liquidity preference and money market adjustment. This serves as an essential type of link between the real and money economy. However, if, as our experience shows, the interest rate appears to be unreliable and weakly related to aggregate investment in our model, the link becomes broken. This happens in our sample although our position may be greatly changed in a less aggregative system. Since liquid assets are lagged in both the consumption and investment equations, these variables are predetermined in forecasting and do not involve the use of the monetary equations.

The role of the classical monetary equation for determination of absolute price and wages is played in our model by the labor market adjustment equation, relating the rate of change of absolute wage rates to unemployment and lagged absolute prices. [1] This is an alternative interpretation of underlying economic forces and should be viewed as an important property of the model.

The principle of absolute price determination can be carried much further. In addition to the relation between absolute wage changes and unemployment, we have many individual markets in which fluctuations in absolute prices are related to excess supplies or demands. Equilibrium theory gives us a rationale for writing demand and supply equations in terms of relative prices, but we have no corresponding rationale for the dynamic processes of market clearance. Our model has no equations of market clearance in the nonmonetary sphere other than that of labor; furthermore, we do not give explicit attention to highly speculative patterns of behavior such as rental real estate and inventories; hence, wage bargaining is the main source of absolute price determination. This would be less true if we were to disaggregate and include many types of market bargaining and speculative behavior.

---

[1] Naturally this statement is subject to the qualification that in multivariate simultaneous equation systems precise lines of causation can usually not be singled out as simply as we have done in the text. We mean that if a homogeneous equation were to replace our bargaining equation, absolute levels of wages and prices would not be determinate in the subsystem splitting off from the monetary equations.

IV. STATISTICAL ESTIMATION OF THE MODEL

METHODS

Detailed treatment of the principles underlying the statistical estimation of our econometric model can be found in other sources. [1]) We shall merely sketch briefly an outline of the approach used and explain some aspects of the computational design not generally available in other references.

At the root of the statistical procedures used in econometrics are the stochastic or probability characteristics of the model. The choice of statistical methods and the reasonableness of that choice depend critically on the stochastic model. The reader has undoubtedly noted that each structural equation of the model, accounting identities aside, has a random disturbance u_{it} attached to it. This is more than a mere formal appendage. Our theory is that we have introduced observable systematic variables into each equation that account for part of the variation in *endogenous* magnitudes. Another part is unaccounted for by our theory of the economic structure. *We have no preconceptions about the size of the unexplained errors; we simply believe that they are accounted for by the laws of chance.* We have not made direct observation of these chance variables, but we do try to make estimates of the properties of their laws of distribution.

We push the theory as far as we think we can manage, with a fairly small number of observable factors. We think that other variables are at work in the economic process but assume them to be very numerous, independent, and *individually* small. Insofar as possible we try to use *a priori* knowledge in specifying the nature of the random disturbances. Some relationships may be thought to be relatively

---

[1]) *Statistical Inference in Dynamic Economic Models*, Cowles Commission Monograph 10, ed. by Tjalling C. Koopmans, (New York: John Wiley and Sons, 1950), *Studies in Econometric Method*, Cowles Commission Monograph 14, ed. by William C. Hood and Tjalling C. Koopmans, (New York: John Wiley and Sons, 1953), L. R. Klein, *A Textbook of Econometrics*, (Evanston: Row, Peterson and Co., 1953).

stable and subject to smaller perturbations than others. Purely exogenous variables are assumed to be independent of the disturbances associated with equations involving endogenous variables. This is reasonable if the exogenous variables are chosen from processes that are not influenced by the economic process. This would certainly be true of climate. It is less true of foreign economic and domestic political variables. We also assume the disturbances to be, timewise, mutually independent, but this is an assumption of convenience and simplification rather than of fact.

In a general sense our theory proceeds as follows: Assume three sets of variables in the sample period $t = 1, 2, \ldots, T$.

$$y_{it} = i\text{-th endogenous variable at time } t.$$
$$z_{it} = i\text{-th exogenous variable at time } t.$$
$$u_{it} = i\text{-th random disturbance at time } t.$$

The structural relations take the form

$$f_i(y_{1t}, \ldots, y_{nt}, y_{1,t-1}, \ldots, y_{n,t-1}, \ldots, y_{1,t-p}, \ldots, y_{n,t-p}, z_{1t}, \ldots, z_{mt}) = u_{it},$$
$$i = 1, 2, \ldots, n,$$
$$t = 1, 2, \ldots, T.$$

The parameters of f_i are the structural characteristics to be estimated in this system of n equations in n endogenous variables and m exogenous variables. The n endogenous variables are lagged up to the p-th order. The unlagged nature of the exogenous variables is purely formal since lagged values of these variables are redefined as new exogenous variables with differing first subscripts.

Assume next that the sample of u_{it} are jointly distributed according to some probability density function

$$p(u_{11}, \ldots, u_{n1}, \ldots, u_{1T}, \ldots, u_{nT}).$$

The assumption of timewise mutual independence would imply a density function of the form

$$[p(u_{1t}, \ldots, u_{nt})]^T.$$

The stricter assumption of complete mutual independence would lead, with identical distributions, to the more special form

$$[p(u_{it})]^{nT}.$$

A theorem of probability theory tells us that if we know the probability distribution of one of two functionally related random variables, we can derive the distribution of the other random variable. This theorem is readily extended to two sets of random variables connected by a system of functional relationships.

Let us look upon our structural equations as a system of relations showing how the random disturbances, u_{it}, are connected to the endogenous variables, y_{it}, given lagged values of endogenous variables, $y_{i,t-j}$, and exogenous variables, z_{it}. Thus, from any distribution of disturbances, we can derive the following type of *conditional* probability density function of the endogenous variables

$$[q(y_{1t}, \ldots, y_{nt}/y_{1,t-1}, \ldots, y_{n,t-1}, \ldots, y_{1,t-p}, \ldots, y_{n,t-p}, z_{1t}, \ldots, z_{mt})]^T.$$

We assume timewise independence in this formulation.

The joint distribution of endogenous variables, derived by the approach outlined above, depends on the structural parameters of the economic system because the structural equations were used in obtaining q from p. We shall choose as our estimates of the parameters, those values which make the probability density $[q]^T$ as large as possible. This maximizes the likelihood of our sample, and we call the estimates so obtained maximum likelihood estimates.

A straightforward application of this principle with no qualifications often leads to very complicated estimating equations for unknown parameters which cannot be solved in large systems unless the investigator has large and expensive computing equipment at his disposal; consequently we use a modified version of this approach known as the *limited information* maximum likelihood method of estimation in contrast to the alternative full information method. In order to explain this method to readers it is necessary to make use of two concepts frequently encountered in modern econometrics – *a priori* restrictions on, and reduced forms of, a structural system.

The general way in which we write structural equations,

$$f_i = u_{it}, \quad i = 1, 2, \ldots, n,$$

suggests that each structural equation would involve all the variables of the system as arguments of the f_i-functions and that each variable would make an independent contribution to each equation. This is the point at which the economist's *a priori* knowledge is called upon to distinguish this equation system from others that may have the same

44

formal appearances, say physical systems or psychological systems. If f_j is to be a structural function representing the behavior of consumers, we may very well be justified in excluding investment as a variable in this equation while including only those factors that have a direct impact on consumer decisions. Every variable does not appear in every equation since the economist's knowledge is used to specify which variables go into which relationships. This can easily be seen to be true in the structural system developed in Chapter II. Each equation in that system involves only the relevant variables to explain particular types of economic behavior described by each relation. Moreover, the separate variables that appear in any given equation do not always play independent roles. In equations of consumer behavior, private and public wage payments are tied together as a sum, meaning that they have the same marginal propensities to consume, yet these two variables are not tied in this fashion in other equations. They are effectively two variables.

Specifications showing which variables go into which equations and how the influences of different variables are tied together in various equations are called restrictions. Therefore, in addition to the abstract formulation of structural equations expressed previously in this section by

$$f_i(y_{1t}, \ldots, y_{nt}, y_{1,t-1}, \ldots, y_{n,t-1}, \ldots, y_{1,t-p}, \ldots, y_{n,t-p}, z_{1t}, \ldots, z_{mt}) = u_{it},$$
$$i = 1, 2, \ldots, n,$$

we have a set of restrictions

$$r_i(a_{i1}, \ldots, a_{is}) = 0, \quad i = 1, 2, \ldots, n.$$

The restrictions, r_i, depend upon the parameters, a, of the structural equations. In linear systems there are as many parameters as different variables in each equation. Absence of a variable is represented by making its associated parameter equal zero. It is important to note that restrictions are placed on each structural equation.

The other concept we want to explain is that of reduced form, a set of equations which expresses each unlagged endogenous variable as a function of purely exogenous or lagged variables alone. Given the system of n equations in n endogenous variables without lags, lagged endogenous variables up to the p-th order, and m exogenous variables, it is possible under known mathematical conditions to derive the equation system

45

$$y_{it} = g_i(y_{1,t-1}, \ldots, y_{n,t-1}, \ldots, y_{1,t-p}, \ldots, y_{n,t-p}, z_{1t}, \ldots, z_{mt}, u_{1t}, \ldots, u_{nt})$$
$$i = 1, 2, \ldots, n, \quad t = 1, 2, \ldots, T.$$

This is the reduced form of the structural system. If the original system is linear, the reduced form can be derived provided the determinant of coefficients of endogenous variables does not vanish. In addition, each reduced form will have a random disturbance, v_{it}, superimposed upon it, where v_{it} is a linear function of the original u_{it}'s. Relatively simple correspondences can be established between the parameters of linear structural equations and the derived linear reduced form equations.

Instead of maximizing the joint probability distribution of the u_{it} (transformed into the joint probability distribution of the endogenous variables by the structural equations) subject to the restriction equations, we may equally well maximize the joint probability distribution of the v_{it} (transformed into the joint probability distribution of the endogenous variables by the reduced form equations) subject to the restriction equations.

We come now to the main point of leading the reader into this digression on restrictions and reduced forms. The method of limited information maximum likelihood estimation, maximizes the joint probability of the v_{it} (transformed into the joint probability distribution of the endogenous variables by the reduced form equations) subject only to the restrictions on some particular structural equation being estimated. It deliberately ignores the restrictions on other structural equations in the system. The joint probability being maximized is, of course, that of v_{it} attached only to reduced form equations associated with endogenous variables in the structural equation being estimated.

Let us try to clarify this approach with an example. The production function in our model is

(7) $\quad (Y + T + D - W_2)_t = \eta_0 + \eta_1[h(N_W - N_G) + N_E + N_F]_t +$
$$+ \eta_2 \frac{K_t + K_{t-1}}{2} + \eta_3 t + u_{7t}.$$

Endogenous variables are Y_t, D_t, $(N_W)_t$ and K_t.
One endogenous variable is lagged, K_{t-1}.

Exogenous variables are T_t, $(W_2)_t$, h_t, $(N_G)_t$, $(N_E)_t$, $(N_F)_t$ and t. One set of restrictions on this equation states that many variables occurring in the system do not appear in this particular relation. For example, the index of agricultural exports is not an explicit variable. In effect, it can be regarded as an additive linear term with a zero coefficient. Another set of restrictions states that the coefficients of several variables are fixed in relation to each other. The coefficients of Y_t, T_t, D_t and $(W_2)_t$ are all plus or minus unity. We even have the nonlinear restriction that the coefficient of h_t is proportional to $(N_W)_t$ and *vice versa*. A convenient way of taking the second set of restrictions into account is to redefine $(Y + T + D - W_2)_t$, $[h(N_W - N_G) + + N_E + N_F]_t$, and $\dfrac{K_t + K_{t-1}}{2}$ as three separate *endogenous* variables. Each of these three endogenous variables is assumed to be associated with a reduced form equation. The joint distribution of the three disturbances attached to each of these reduced forms is maximized subject to the restrictions which state that certain variables are missing from equation (7). Restrictions on the other structural equations of the system are not taken into account.

The effect of this procedure of ignoring information is to change our parameter estimation problem from the solution of one large system of nonlinear equations into the comparatively easier solution of several smaller systems involving nothing more difficult than ordinary matrix calculations. In spite of the fact that restrictions on other equations in the system are ignored, we still capture the spirit of simultaneity in economic relations by having to specify and make use of variables in the entire system but not in a particular equation being estimated. By ignoring some information, we lose efficiency in the statistical sense; nevertheless we do not introduce bias into our statistical estimates because we take some account of the fact that economic processes occur simultaneously.

The precise steps involved in computing numerical estimates by the method of limited information shall not be taken up here. The references listed at the beginning of this section give all the necessary details. Suffice it to note that the unique features of limited information methods, on the one hand, enabling us to estimate one equation at a time and, on the other, tying this estimate to the entire system of equations, require a few words of comment in order that the reader will have a fuller interpretation of our results.

The first stage in the derivation of limited information estimates requires the computation of the variance-covariance matrix of residuals from the least-squares regression of each endogenous variable in the equation being considered on all the predetermined variables (lagged endogenous and exogenous) in the system. These are *reduced form* equations described above. In a system as large as, or larger than, that we are dealing with, the number of predetermined variables is high. We may have the difficulty of solving a large number of simultaneous equations, and we may have the more embarrassing difficulty of not having enough degrees of freedom to carry out this first stage of the estimation process. With adequate equipment, the former difficulty can be overcome. The latter is not as easily avoided.

We are familiar with the proposition that a linear function with n unknown parameters can be exactly fitted to n observations. The residuals are zero. If the number of unknown parameters is larger than the number of observations, the results of fitting are indeterminate. If we were to use every predetermined variable in the system and follow the principles of the limited information method, we should find ourselves confronted with an indeterminacy of this type. Fortunately it can be shown that the properties of consistency, in the statistical sense, of the limited information method are preserved even if not all the predetermined variables in the system are used in this step.

The more predetermined variables from other equations one is able to make use of in the estimation of any single equation, the more one is able to bring out the equation system nature of the economic process. In sufficiently large samples, it would be better to make use of as many predetermined variables as possible, but what principles are to be used in choosing a selective set when all cannot be used?

Predetermined variables are prime movers of the endogenous magnitudes; therefore, one should, if possible, make use of the most important predetermined variables – those that account most for economic fluctuations in the model. If some predetermined variable has changed little in the past; as measured by a coefficient of variation, say; and is expected to change little in the future it could be a candidate

48

for exclusion. Among highly intercorrelated predetermined variables, it usually suffices to select a single representative variable.

The nature of the estimation method is such that predetermined variables occurring in explicit form in any particular equation must evidently be used in the estimation of that equation. For mutual consistency and also for economies in computation it is desirable to choose a single set of predetermined variables applicable to the estimation of any equation in the system. [1]) An element of arbitrariness can be eliminated in this way. Because of restrictions on a system, it often happens that the number of predetermined variables explicitly occurring in any equation is less than the number of different predetermined variables in the system. In the model for which estimates are presented below, we have used all explicitly occurring predetermined variables plus the most important among those remaining. The only exception to this rule applies to special equations which occur in a form with only one endogenous variable and several predetermined variables. For these cases, one can do no better than make single-equation least-squares estimates. There are a few instances of this approach in our model; otherwise we have used a single set of predetermined variables in the limited information estimation of the equations.

Suppose that we use as many as 15–20 predetermined variables in limited information estimation of aggregative econometric models. This many predetermined factors account for such a large part of variation in any of the endogenous variables, that inclusion or exclusion of a few more has little effect on the variance-covariance matrix of residuals. After as many as 10 predetermined variables have been used, provided they include some obviously strategic factors, we can account for a large part of the variability in most endogenous variables considered. The contributions of other predetermined variables, *at this first step of the computations*, are largely marginal. The remaining steps in the computational procedure do not involve similar matters of decision.

With a fixed set of predetermined variables selected in advance of limited information estimation, it is possible to make various experi-

---

[1]) In the estimation of an earlier system, blocks of predetermined variables were used for different blocks of equations. See L. R. Klein, *Economic Fluctuations in the United States, 1921–1941*, (New York: John Wiley and Sons, 1950).

mental computations. The most burdensome step is the first, involving the inversion of the matrix of moments of all predetermined variables used. If we can perform this operation once and use the results repeatedly, it becomes possible to experiment with various alternative hypotheses, changing the composition of endogenous and predetermined variables in a given equation. A relatively small amount of computation is needed for experimental alterations. The inability to experiment cheaply has been a serious drawback to modern econometric methods, but we have designed our computations to facilitate experimentation as much as possible.

In the estimation of our model given in section II, we have, with three exceptions, used a single set of predetermined variables for the estimation of each equation. Equation (14), the empirical relation between short and long run interest rates, and equation (15), the money market adjustment equation, are both written in a form immediately adapted to single-equation least squares estimation. Each has only one unlagged endogenous variable. Equation (2), the investment function, was originally not written as a special case, but empirical study and experimentation with different forms led us to treat investment as a function of predetermined variables alone, although this is only a temporary solution pending further studies of disaggregated variables.

Empirical Results

Except for the three mentioned above, the equations of the model were estimated by the method of limited information using the following set of predetermined variables:

$$C_{t-1} = \text{lagged consumer expenditures in 1939 dollars.}$$

$$(L_1)_{t-1} = \text{lagged deflated, year-end liquid assets held by households.}$$

$$(N_P)_t = \text{number of persons in the United States.}$$

$$(P+A+D-T_P-T_A)_{t-1} = \text{lagged deflated, disposable non-wage income plus depreciation and corporate savings.}$$

$$K_{t-1} = \text{lagged year-end stock of fixed capital in 1939 dollars.}$$

$$(L_2)_{t-1} = \text{lagged deflated, year-end liquid assets held by enterprises.}$$

$$(P_C - T_C - S_P)_{t-1} = \text{lagged deflated corporate dividend payments.}$$

$$B_{t-1} = \text{lagged deflated, year-end accumulated corporate savings.}$$

$$(Y + T + D - W_2)_{t-1} = \text{lagged private gross national product in 1939 dollars.}$$

$$t = \text{time trend in years.}$$

$$p_{t-1} - p_{t-2} = \text{lagged first differences in the general price index.}$$

$$(F_I)_{t-1} = \text{lagged imports of goods and services in 1939 dollars.}$$

$$(W_1 + W_2 + P - S_P - T_W - T_P)_{t-1} = \text{lagged deflated nonfarm disposable income.}$$

$$(F_A)_t = \text{index of agricultural exports.}$$

$$(G + F_E)_t = \text{government expenditures plus exports of goods and services.}$$

The estimated model over the sample period 1929–41; 1946–50 in billions of dollars, millions of persons, and indexes based on the year 1939 is

(1) $C_t = -34.5 + 0.62(W_1 + W_2 - T_W)_t + 0.46(P - S_P - T_P)_t +$
 (7.7) (0.04) (0.03)

 $+ 0.39 \ (A - T_A)_t + 0.23 C_{t-1} + 0.024(L_1)_{t-1} + 0.36(N_P)_t$
 (0.025) (0.05) (0.02) $\phantom{(L_1)_{t-1}}$ (0.08)

$$\delta^2 / S^2 = 2.2$$

(2) $I_t = -16.8 + 0.76(P + A + D - T_P - T_A)_{t-1} - 0.14 K_{t-1} + 0.14(L_2)_{t-1}$
 (4.5) (0.17) $\phantom{(P + A + D - T_P - T_A)_{t-1}}$ (0.08) (0.10)

$$\delta^2 / S^2 = 2.3$$

(3) $(S_P)_t = -2.42 + 0.86(P_C - T_C)_t - 0.30(P_C - T_C - S_P)_{t-1} - 0.014 B_{t-1}$
 (0.81) (0.04) (0.20) $\phantom{(P_C - T_C - S_P)_{t-1}}$ (0.016)

$$\delta^2 / S^2 = 1.9$$

(4) $(P_C)_t = -8.34 + 0.71 P_t$
$\qquad$ (0.53) $\quad$ (0.02)

$$\delta^2/S^2 = 1.4$$

(5) $D_t = 11.46 + 0.14 \dfrac{K_t + K_{t-1}}{2}$
$\qquad$ (0.36) $\quad$ (0.08)

$$\delta^2/S^2 = 0.30$$

(6) $(W_1)_t = -2.70 + 0.36(Y + T + D - W_2)_t +$
$\qquad$ (1.05) $\quad$ (0.04)

$$+ 0.14(Y + T + D - W_2)_{t-1} + 0.16t$$
$\qquad\qquad$ (0.03) $\qquad\qquad\qquad\qquad\qquad$ (0.08)

$$\delta^2/S^2 = 2.0$$

(7) $(Y+T+D-W_2)_t = -31.98 + 2.31[h(N_W - N_G) + N_E + N_F]_t +$
$\qquad\qquad$ (7.3) $\quad$ (0.18)

$$+ 0.076 \dfrac{K_t + K_{t-1}}{2} + 1.90t$$
$\qquad\qquad$ (0.06) $\qquad\qquad\qquad$ (0.15)

$$\delta^2/S^2 = 1.4$$

(8) $w_t - w_{t-1} = 4.11 - 0.75(N - N_W - N_E - N_F)_t +$
$\qquad\qquad$ (4.83) $\quad$ (0.63)

$$+ 0.56(p_{t-1} - p_{t-2}) + 0.56t$$
$\qquad\qquad$ (0.30) $\qquad\qquad\qquad$ (0.26)

$$\delta^2/S^2 = 2.4$$

(9) $(F_I)_t = 2.09 + 0.0087(W_1 + W_2 + P + A - T_W - T_P - T_A)_t \dfrac{p_t}{(p_I)_t} +$
$\qquad$ (0.65) (0.0057)

$$+ 0.24(F_I)_{t-1}$$
$\qquad\qquad$ (0.12)

$$\delta^2/S^2 = 1.6$$

(10) $A_t = -4.53 + 0.25(W_1 + W_2 + P - S_P - T_W - T_P)_t -$
$\qquad$ (1.48) (0.09)

$$- 0.13(W_1 + W_2 + P - S_P - T_W - T_P)_{t-1} + 0.0096(F_A)_t$$
$\qquad\qquad$ (0.11) $\qquad\qquad\qquad\qquad\qquad$ (0.014)

$$\delta^2/S^2 = 1.5$$

(12) $(L_1)_t = 0.14(W_1 + W_2 + P + A - T_W - T_P - S_P - T_A)_t +$

$$+ 75.0 \; (i_L - 2.0)_t^{-0.84 \; (0.03)}$$
$$(16.6)$$

$$\delta^2/S^2 = 0.73 \quad \text{(for the logarithmic form of residuals)}$$

(13) $(L_2)_t = -0.77 + 0.24(W_1)_t - 0.69(i_S)_t - 0.27(p_t - p_{t-1}) + 0.64(L_2)_{t-1}$
$\quad\quad\quad (1.43)\;(0.05)\quad\quad (0.31)\quad\quad\;\; (0.09)\quad\quad\quad\; (0.08)$

$$\delta^2/S^2 = 2.0$$

(14) $(i_L)_t = 2.66 + 0.46(i_S)_{t-3} + 0.23(i_S)_{t-5} \quad\quad \delta^2/S^2 = 0.9$
$\quad\quad\quad\; (0.17)\quad (0.10)\quad\quad\quad (0.10)$

(15) $100 \dfrac{(i_S)_t - (i_S)_{t-1}}{(i_S)_{t-1}} = 6.42 - 0.55R \quad\quad \delta^2/S^2 = 1.3$
$\quad\quad\quad\quad\quad\quad\quad\quad\quad\;\; (8.52)\quad (0.31)$

(16) $C_t + I_t + G_t + (F_E)_t - (F_I)_t = Y_t + T_t + D_t$

(17) $(W_1)_t + (W_2)_t + P_t + A_t = Y_t$

(18) $h_t \dfrac{w_t}{p_t} (N_W)_t = (W_1)_t + (W_2)_t$

(19) $K_t - K_{t-1} = I_t - D_t$

(20) $B_t - B_{t-1} = (S_P)_t$

Below each estimated parameter, in parentheses, is the standard error of the estimate. This gives us a measure of statistical reliability. Also each stochastic equation is assumed to have a set of mutually independent disturbances. The statistic δ^2/S^2 for each estimated equation is designed to show the presence or absence of serial correlation in the residuals for each equation and thus provide an indicator of the degree of fulfillment of the above assumption about the disturbances. The expected value of δ^2/S^2 is 2.1 and numerical estimates in the neighborhood of this figure indicate a significant lack of serial correlation in the residuals. Values below 1.25 suggest the presence of serial correlation in the residuals.

The separate contributions of each variable, the calculated series being "explained" in each equation, the observed series being "explained" in each equation, and the discrepancies between calculated

53

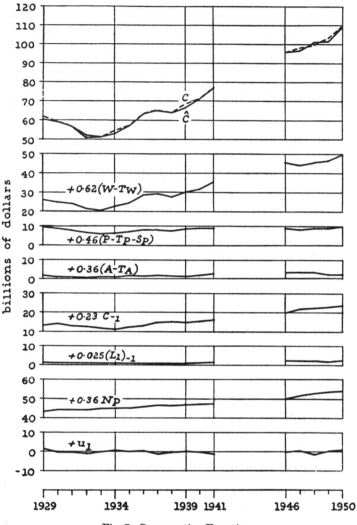

Fig. 7. Consumption Equation

and observed values (residuals) are plotted in Figures 7–20. In successive panels after the first, we present the numerical value of each variable multiplied by its respective coefficient. In the bottom panel, we give the residuals. These can also be ascertained from the top panel showing the calculated and observed values of left hand variables in equations

54

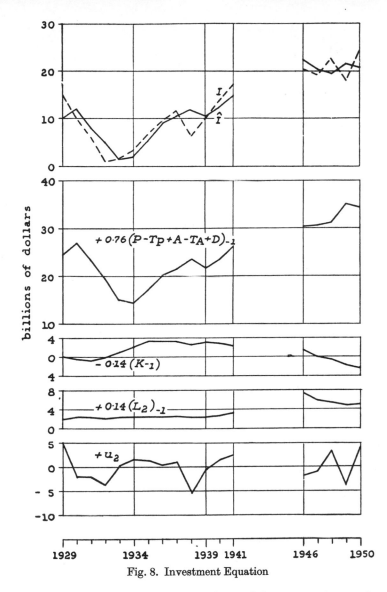

Fig. 8. Investment Equation

(1)–(15). The calculated values are denoted by a superior mark, $\wedge$, over the variable. These Figures are useful in showing the overall correlations and the individual contributions of each variable to this correlation.

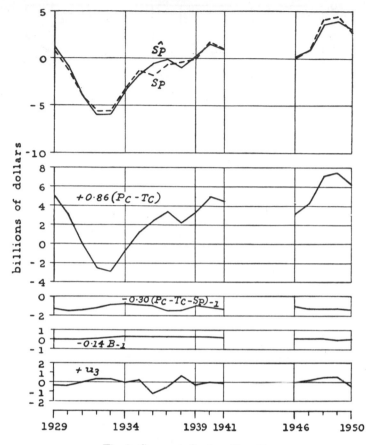

Fig. 9. Corporate Savings Equation

The reader should note some discrepancies between the structure of the model as developed earlier from a priori as well as statistical considerations and the structure estimated in the empirical equations. Within particular samples of information we rarely find that all details of a priori analysis stand up against the facts of real life. Some of the differences between the theoretical and empirical models found here are altered below when observations for 1951 and 1952 are added to the sample and the parameters reestimated. To some extent, we developed our thoughts as we worked on the data and were thus able to incorporate certain features in the later but not in the first set of

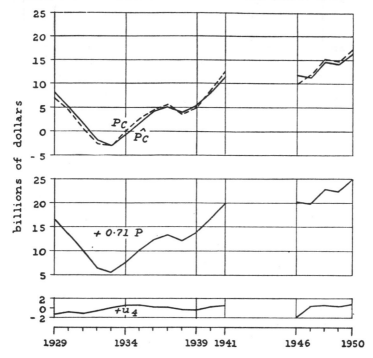

Fig. 10. Relation of Corporate Profits to Nonwage Nonfarm Income

estimates. The computational procedure is somewhat difficult and lengthy; hence, it does not pay to make some minor changes until we come to a situation in which computations have to made again for a variety of weighty reasons.

Remarks on the Consumption Equation

A large number of variables are used in the empirical estimates of (1), and some may wonder at the success of obtaining as many coefficients of the degree of reliability shown. Our sample presents the same difficulties encountered by others, namely, that intercorrelation among the different components of income masks separate contributions of each component towards the explanation of spending, behavior. To avoid this difficulty and estimate the equation with some effect of income distribution shown, we made use of estimates from sample survey data. In the Surveys of Consumer Finances, we are able to

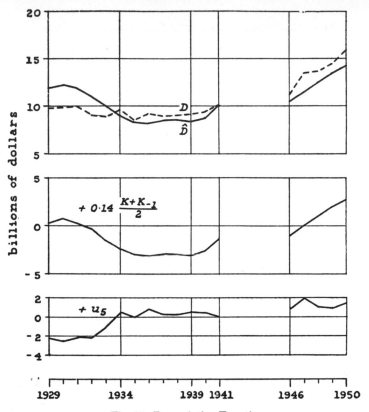

Fig. 11. Depreciation Equation

distinguish between three types of consumer units – farmers; business owners; and nonfarm, nonbusiness units. For individual units we have, in these data, separate estimates of savings and income. Corresponding estimates of savings at the aggregative level are not available. We have estimated the marginal propensities to save for each of the three groups and fixed the coefficients in (1) so that *ratios* among all pairs of the three marginal propensities were equal to the ratios estimated from survey data. Symbolically, instead of estimating three parameters in the partial expression

$$a_1(W_1+W_2-T_W)_t+a_2(P-S_P-T_P)_t+a_3(A-T_A)_t,$$

we first estimate from the survey sample

$$\frac{a_2}{a_1} \quad \text{and} \quad \frac{a_3}{a_1},$$

58

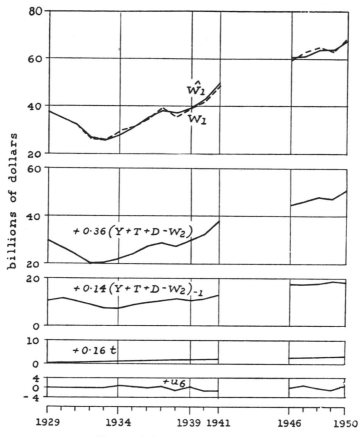

Fig. 12. Labor Demand Equation

following with the use of time series data to estimate a_1 in

$$a_1\left[(W_1+W_2-T_W)_t+\left(\frac{\hat{a}_2}{a_1}\right)(P-S_P-T_P)_t+\left(\frac{\hat{a}_3}{a_1}\right)(A-T_A)_t\right].$$

Survey estimates of the ratios are denoted by

$$\left(\frac{\hat{a}_2}{a_1}\right) \quad \text{and} \quad \left(\frac{\hat{a}_3}{a_1}\right).$$

In effect, we define a new variable which is a particular linear combination of three variables and estimate a single coefficient of this new variable.

59

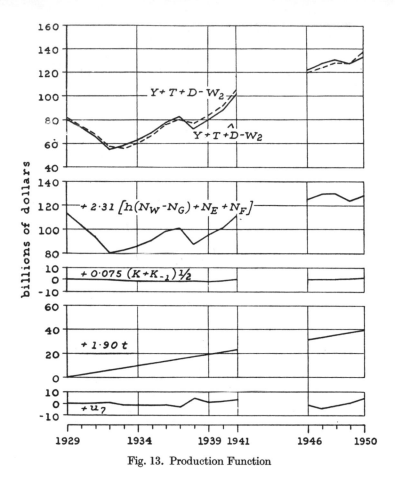

Fig. 13. Production Function

The survey estimates were not made from simple two-dimensional correlations between savings and income for each of the three groups. The marginal propensities for the three groups were determined from multivariate savings equations with fixed values assigned to all variables except savings and income. [1] There is evidence that the survey estimates are not merely applicable to the postwar years in

---

[1] The equations are presented in L. R. Klein, "Statistical Estimation of Economic Relations from Survey Data," *Contributions of Survey Methods to Economics*, (New York: Columbia University Press, 1954).

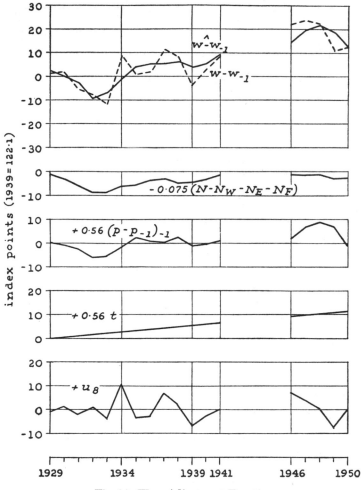

Fig. 14. Wage Adjustment Equation

which the surveys were conducted. From other surveys conducted in the prewar years we find similar ratios for the farm and nonfarm groups, although we are not able to single out businessmen in the earlier period. The postwar surveys used report only on money income of farmers, but there is evidence from a study made in 1941 that the marginal propensity to save is approximately the same

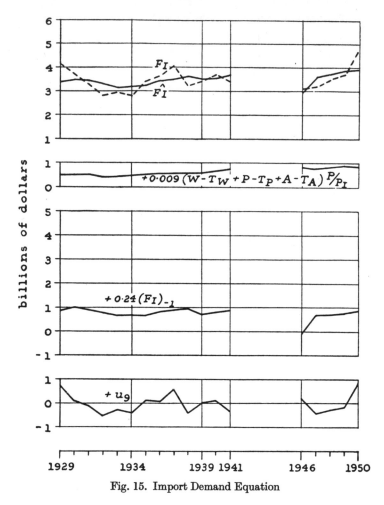

Fig. 15. Import Demand Equation

whether one uses money or total (money plus income in kind) income for farmers. [1])

In our equation with the lagged value of consumption used to show the influence of the past on present behavior, the conventional measures of the marginal propensity to consume are obscured. They are not 0.62, 0.46, and 0.39 respectively. These are merely estimates of short

[1]) *Rural Family Spending and Saving in Wartime*, U.S. Dept. of Agriculture, miscellaneous publication No. 500, June, 1943.

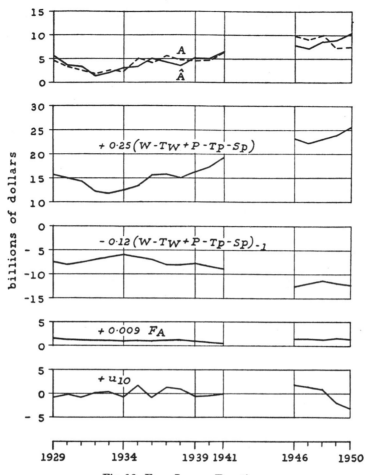

Fig. 16. Farm Income Equation

run marginal propensities. The long run coefficients which would be obtained in equilibrium if consumption were to settle down to a static level,

$$C_t = C_{t-1},$$

are obtained by dividing each coefficient by $(1 - 0.23) = 0.77$. Thus the long run marginal propensities are

$$\frac{0.62}{0.77} = 0.81,$$

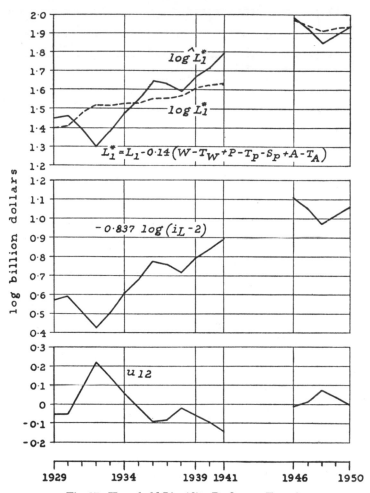

Fig. 17. Household Liquidity Preference Equation

$$\frac{0.46}{0.77} = 0.60,$$

$$\frac{0.39}{0.77} = 0.51.$$

These are more in agreement with values usually employed in analysis. Both the level of liquid asset holdings and population exhibit a

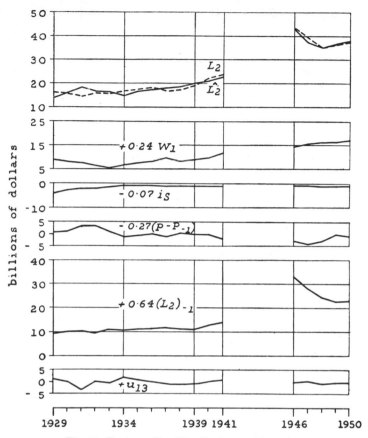

Fig. 18. Business Liquidity Preference Equation

similar upward growth and are intercorrelated, although population does not have the same jump over the war years as does liquid asset holdings. Intercorrelation probably makes the coefficient of liquid assets small because if population is omitted from the equation, this coefficient is estimated at 0.064. This latter estimate is more in agreement with independent survey estimates than is the value 0.024 in (1). The addition of two sampling errors to 0.024 would not bring it in range of the survey estimate. A slight upward bias in the survey estimate is caused by the fact that currency holdings are not included in the concept of liquid assets used there, but we are inclined to attribute

65

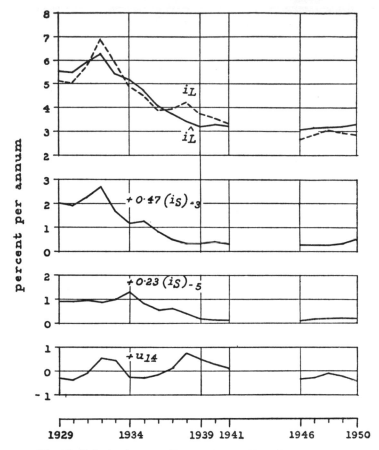

Fig. 19. Relation between Short and Long Term Interest Rates

a definite downward bias to our estimate in (1) because of inter-correlation.

REMARKS ON THE INVESTMENT EQUATION

In the general discussion of the investment equation we allowed for a lag in, or dynamic aspects of, behavior by contemplating both current and past values of profit (nonwage income) as variables. Most information we can gather from outside sources would suggest an average lag of less than one year between investment and profits, accounted for by the lapse of time between orders and deliveries or production

66

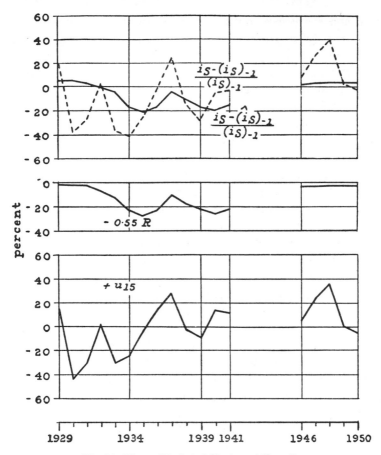

Fig. 20. Money Market Adjustment Equation

period of capital goods. The fixed lag of a year expressed in equation (2) is purely an empirical result, indicating that we have not found reasonable estimates of the equations with unlagged earnings appearing simultaneously with lagged earnings.

We come to a similar conclusion with respect to the rate of interest in the investment function. In using our highly aggregative measure of investment, we find no reasonable empirical results for the effect of interest. In all possible combinations with current nonwage income, lagged nonwage income, and long term bond yield we obtain estimated coefficients with signs contrary to advance expectations, large sampling

67

errors, and sometimes impossibly large coefficients. To some extent these results follow from our failure to distinguish among inventories, construction, and equipment. In a larger model we may expect to find the short term interest rate significant in inventory outlays, the long term interest rate significant in construction outlays, and unlagged income significant in either inventory or equipment outlays.

We are not following the rule of automatically rejecting equations in which some coefficients are not at least two or three times as large as their sampling error, nor are we rejecting equations with coefficients of the "wrong" sign, *provided these coefficients do not differ significantly from zero*. We are, however, rejecting estimated equations which appear to have empirically unstable coefficients due to the presence of certain particular variables. For example, in the investment equation, we expect the coefficient of nonwage disposable income to lie somewhere between 0.5 and 1.0. Many past aggregative studies, cross section sample studies, and separate industry studies lead us to expect this. In the present sample, we have obtained explosive coefficients of current and lagged income (2.1 and −1.4) if both variables are included together. Their sum is nearly the same as the single coefficient of lagged income in (2), but separately they have become magnified in an unstable manner when treated together. At the same time, the coefficients of capital and liquid assets change sign. A similar scrambling of coefficients by sign and magnitude occurs if the average bond yield is included as an additional variable. On the other hand, our empirical estimate of the pure lagged form shows both reasonableness and stability. In some forecasting situations, the pure lag seems to be incorrect but it gives a good approximation to actual investment, on the average, over the sample observations. The fact that the coefficients of capital and liquid assets both have relatively large sampling errors does not lead us to reject this empirical function.

Remarks on the Relation between Corporate Profits and Nonwage Nonfarm Income and on the Depreciation Equation

In both equations (4) and (5), some variables mentioned already are not included. In (4) it would seem reasonable to include both current and lagged values of nonwage nonfarm income, but we encounter the familiar problem of explosive coefficients if both variables are simultaneously used.

In (5), we did not consider using the current level of private production as an added variable at the time the first calculations were made. The reader can readily see that the sample residuals from (5) show high serial correlation. Extrapolation of this equation shows a bias for recent years. As will be seen below, these deficiencies are mitigated when private output is actually included as an additional variable in the recalculations of the model through the year 1952.

REMARKS ON THE PRODUCTION FUNCTION

Although the coefficient of capital has a relatively large sampling error, it is positive – something which is not often found in empirical estimates of highly aggregative production functions. In anticipation of later results, we might say that this coefficient is much improved in terms of reliability when the years 1951 and 1952 are added to the sample.

The production function has variable elasticities of output per factor input. On the average for the entire sample period, labor input shows increasing returns to scale; i.e. the elasticity exceeds unity. In recent years, however, the elasticity is estimated at a level smaller than unity. Similar elasticity measures cannot be estimated for capital, since the base value of this variable is not known. It is estimated as an inseparable part of the constant term in the equation.

The trend in productivity is simply linear, but there is some reason to believe that productivity grows at a faster pace in this country. However, if quadratic trends are used in this equation, some of the other parameter estimates become unstable; hence we draw the line, empirically, at the linear trend.

REMARKS ON THE AGRICULTURAL INCOME DETERMINATION EQUATION

While it is reasonable to assume that both nonagricultural income and relative prices would be of importance in determining the level of agricultural income, we find no reasonable empirical results using relative prices as a separate variable. Our empirical estimate of (10) is written slightly differently than the preceding text version. The empirical equation relates A_t (net agricultural income deflated by the general price level) to $(W_1+W_2+P-S_P-T_W-T_P)_t$ (nonagricultural disposable income deflated by the general price level). In later computations, we shall deflate both current price flows by the agricultural price level. This will automatically give some influence to relative prices.

The difference in sign and magnitude of the two coefficients of nonagricultural income in (10) – current and lagged values respectively – can be interpreted as indicating a positive effect for the current level (0.12) and a positive effect for the rate of change (0.13).

Since no empirical significance is attached to relative prices between the farm and nonfarm sectors, there is no need to include an equation for agricultural price determination in the system.

REMARKS ON THE HOUSEHOLD AND BUSINESS LIQUIDITY PREFERENCE EQUATIONS

In the case of nonbusiness cash holdings we have estimated the transactions coefficient as the minimal ratio of personal currency and checking deposits to disposable personal income. The "floor" to the long term interest rate in this equation is arbitrarily set at 2.0 percent. This value seemed to give a somewhat better empirical relation than others in the immediate neighborhood.

The transactions coefficient in the business liquidity preference equation is the same whether estimated as the minimal ratio of currency and checking accounts to the wage bill or as a free coefficient in a linear equation.

NOTE ON COMPUTATIONAL METHODS

The heavy calculating burden of equation system estimation, which has limited the flexibility of econometric research and enabled least-squares estimation to retain its popularity, is gradually being overcome. In the course of our research on the econometric model presented here, new methods of handling limited-information maximum likelihood calculations have been developed. We have had the use of the IBM Card Programmed Calculator of the Tabulating Service of the University of Michigan, a punched-card electronic computer, specially wired for matrix operations. In our first estimation of the model,

70

the CPC was used to invert the 15×15 matrix, Z, of moments of the predetermined variables and obtain matrix products of the form $YZ^{-1}Y'$, a major step in parameter estimation. (Y = moment matrix between endogenous and predetermined variables.) For the second estimation (see below pp. 90–92) all the moments were computed on the CPC. In addition, program decks were developed and used to handle on the CPC the entire series of calculations necessary to obtain the estimates of parameters and their sampling errors, and the annual residuals of the structural equations. Once the program decks were prepared, it was easy to experiment with alternative forms of the equations of the model. Also, future re-estimation of the model, as the sample period is extended, is no longer an overwhelming task.

V. EXTRAPOLATION AND FORECASTING

SOME PRINCIPLES OF FORECASTING

The severest test of any theory is that of its ability to predict. Our equation system presents a theory of economic behavior in the aggregate. We have fitted the model to the sample, and although it may be an achievement to find a structural system which does fit the observed facts, we cannot be satisfied with the performance of the system solely with reference to the sample data.

In a broad sense, we mean, by prediction, the ability of the equations to explain aggregate economic behavior for sets of observations outside the sample. We have approached this problem empirically from two points of view. In an *ex-post* sense we may insert observed and essentially correct values of predetermined variables in the model and solve it algebraically for the values of endogenous variables in the forecast period. One interested in the degree to which our model represents a true picture of behavior should base his judgment of performance on this ex-post type of extrapolation. This is a case of testing the model outside the confines of the sample and determining how well it fits actual observations when there is no statistical forcing towards conformity.

The data describing our modern economy are continuously being processed and refined. At best, there is a lag of one to six months for the reporting of most economic series. The first estimates are preliminary and are often revised a few months after first publication. It may require a lapse of time as long as two years before a careful *ex-post* test of extrapolation can be made. At somewhat longer intervals comprehensive revisions are made. These may affect estimates for both the sample and forecast period.

True prediction, or forecasting, in an *ex-ante* sense cannot await the publication of corrected economic data, and we may pose the question: How well can econometric models serve us in prediction if we have only imperfect estimates of predetermined variables in advance of the forecast period? Lagged variables within the predetermined set are usually not known exactly for an advance forecast unless the lag is one of a few time periods. For example, in using an annual model to forecast the year $t + 1$ in November or December of year t, we do not yet have annual estimates of data for the year t. These estimates are needed for the variables lagged one year in the model. Towards the end of the t-th year, we can make estimates of the lagged variables to be used in forecasting the $t + 1$st year on the basis of observations reported in the first nine or ten months. However, these estimates are subject to error. Not only do they depend on data not yet available for the last month or two, they also depend on inexact, preliminary estimates for earlier quarters of the t-th year.

Lagged variables present problems in *ex-ante* forecasting, but contemporary exogenous variables are sometimes even less firmly established for the future, forecast period. Among those more accurately determined are some population trends that move slowly and smoothly. They can be accurately estimated one year in advance, although in some instances not for more distant time periods. Government variables are fixed by various laws and budget commitments. Foreign variables depend on affairs of the outside world. We have relied on expert opinion of people in close touch with foreign developments, but perhaps have not properly allowed for repercussions of the United States on world markets. To a large extent, our exports in recent years have depended on overseas grants made by the government, and these can be estimated about as well as general government expenditures.

In spite of the fact that some contemporaneous exogenous variables are subject to uncertainty for the forecast period, we can make useful statements about alternative hypothetical states of the system that would be realized under different assumed conditions. If the *ex-post* extrapolations have shown a system to give a good explanation of economic behavior, we can then place a measure of reliance on the use of this system to show what *would* happen if exogenous variables *were* to be placed at particular assumed levels. We might show, for example, the sensitivity of aggregate activity to variations in government tax-expenditure plans. This is a form of *ex-ante* forecasting and may be a more useful econometric application than pure forecasts of the expected levels of endogenous variables.

We have spoken of calculation of the forecast values as a mechanical problem of algebra. Given a system with statistically estimated coefficients, we substitute values of all predetermined variables and solve for unlagged endogenous variables. Our solution is a set of unique values satisfying the equation system, yet there are implicit assumptions involved that should lead us to surround this set of numbers by regions of uncertainty. We have statistical models based on probability calculations; therefore our forecast estimates are probabilistic and not exact values. Errors arise because the numerical coefficients in our equations are not firmly established from samples of infinite size (sampling error), because the system does not function exactly as our equations say it does (disturbances), and because we do not know the correct values of predetermined variables at the time of forecast.

The theory of forecasting error associated with estimated linear stochastic equations is fairly well developed. In an equation of the form

$$y_t = \sum_{i=1}^{n} \alpha_i z_{it} + v_{it},$$

the variance of the forecasted value of y_T in time period T (outside the sample) is given by the expression

$$S_{y_T}^2 = \sum_{i,j} S_{a_i a_j}^2 (z_{iT} - \bar{z}_i)(z_{jT} - \bar{z}_j) + S_v^2.$$

$S_{a_i a_j}^2$ = covariance of the *estimates* of α_i and α_j.
z_{iT} = value of i-th predetermined variable in forecast period T.
$\bar{z}_i$ = sample mean of i-th predetermined variable.
S_v^2 = *estimate* of variance of disturbances.

The forecast equation is derived as a solution to the linear structural system; that is why it is assumed to be expressible in a form with one endogenous variable as a function of predetermined variables alone. This means, however, that the α_i are not the original structural parameters. They are functions of them. The variances and covariances of the a_i (estimates of the α_i) will depend on the variances and covariances of the estimates of the original structural parameters. Among these, we lack estimates of the covariances between coefficients occurring in different structural equations. They are not obtainable

74

by our method of statistical estimation although they would be in the case of full maximum likelihood estimates.

The standard-error-of-forecast formula given above assumes that the z_{iT} are exactly known for the forecast period. Error in the estimation of these should be added to the forecast error. Practically the only possibility of estimating such error would be to canvass expert opinion of data-collecting statisticians at the time of forecast preparation.

In our forecasts, we have not estimated $S^2_{\nu_T}$ because of the difficulties mentioned above. In addition, the nonlinearities of our system make such estimation even more difficult. We do, however, ask the reader to bear in mind the probabilistic nature of our forecasts or extrapolations even though we do not measure the numerical probability limit involved.

In deriving the algebraic point forecasts, we solve the system of estimated equations as though there were no disturbances. In the above example this is equivalent to assuming the expected value of v_t to be zero, which it is, in fact, if the structural system is linear and if each equation is disturbed by a random variable with zero mean. Two reasons must be mentioned, however, for not making forecast estimates from our nonlinear system by assuming all disturbance terms to be zero. Although disturbances are individually zero, on the average, their covariation need not be zero on the average. In a linear structural model, the error term of the final forecast equation (expressing endogenous variables as a linear function of predetermined variables alone) is a linear function of error terms in the original structural equations, but in a nonlinear system this result is not true. The forecast equations will depend upon nonlinear functions of the separate disturbances, and, in general, the estimated covariances of these disturbances will have to be taken into account. However, in some experimental calculations with the present model, it was found that these estimated covariances had no perceptible effect on the forecasts; hence, we have not revised our treatment of the error terms on that account.

The other reason for not assuming all error terms to be precisely zero in forecasting is that they may serially correlated. In our probability model for structural estimation, we assume mutual inde-

75

pendence among disturbances occurring at different time periods. We make this assumption for convenience, knowing that it may be violated to some extent empirically, but we refine our equations in the hopes of realizing this basic independence assumption as closely as possible. The main form of lack of independence is thought to be serial correlation of disturbances. If we have not fully realized our assumption we may guard against possible serial correlation of disturbances in forecasting by attempting to correct our forecasts for it. This may be done by estimating the serial correlation of residuals from the fitted model during the sample period.

Define the residuals from the model's final forecast equation as

$$y_t - \sum_{i=1}^{n} a_i z_{it} = r_t.$$

If the residuals are serially correlated, we have

$$r_t = b r_{t-1},$$

in which b is the large sample serial correlation coefficient of the first order. If we assume the disturbances v_t to satisfy a first order autoregressive scheme

$$v_t = \beta v_{t-1} + w_t,$$

b is an estimate of β. In forecasting from a system of this type, we correct for serial correlation by substituting the autoregressive equation for r_t into the estimated forecast equation to get

$$y_t - \sum_{i=1}^{n} a_i z_{it} = b r_{t-1}.$$

Observing that

$$r_{t-1} = y_{t-1} - \sum_{i=1}^{n} a_i z_{i,t-1},$$

we get

$$y_t = b y_{t-1} + \sum_{i=1}^{n} a_i (z_{it} - b z_{i,t-1}).$$

This is the equation to be used in forecasting.

In case $b = 1$, i.e., perfect large sample serial correlation of residuals, we notice that the transformed forecast equation is

$$y_t - y_{t-1} = \sum_{i=1}^{n} a_i (z_{it} - z_{i,t-1})$$

or

$$\Delta y_t = \sum_{i=1}^{n} a_i \Delta z_{it}.$$

This equation transforms our original variables to first differences, and is a logical forecasting equation to use if we expect our errors in period t to be exactly the same as in period $t-1$. If the autoregressive coefficient is unity, this is what we should expect. This is a frequent forecasting device. Sometimes people think that they can forecast the amount of *change* without being able to forecast the *level* accurately. If a constant bias were present, this situation would prevail.

We have experimented with various types of forecasting approaches and suggest neither an assumption that all disturbances are at their mean values (zero) nor any simple autoregressive transformations of variables in forecast equations. Our preferred procedure is to compute the residuals of all structural equations and make a special study of their time patterns in recent period, say, the last five years in annual models. Persistent biases are investigated. These would be indicated by a series of four or five consecutive residuals of the same sign and similar magnitude for the last observation periods. If there is *independent* information to confirm the existence of a bias and if we think it will continue into the forecast period, we use the latest estimate of the residuals as a positive or negative additive constant in the equation system in place of the zero value for the disturbance. It may be emphasized that structural estimation makes this approach possible.

Our external information may consist of results from sample surveys. If our investment equation has been consistently underestimating capital formation in recent years and if surveys of business firms indicate high prospective outlays for the forecast period, we would raise this equation by the amount of the latest estimate of the residual.

The selective assignment of nonzero disturbances in our original structural equations is deemed preferable to any mechanical scheme such as always assuming all disturbances to be zero (their mean values) during the forecast period, serially related by the autoregressive equation satisfied by the sample residuals, or serially related with an autoregressive parameter equal to unity. If we are to develop a truly flexible technique of econometric forecasting, in contrast to any

77

rigid or mechanical method, we must adopt an approach that permits the use of external information. In forecasting we shall always be confronted with up-to-the-minute developments, not reflected in the model and not necessarily persistent for many time periods, but of extreme importance in the forecast situation. We are not, however, leaving this flexible econometric method open to personal judgment. On the basis of the outside information, we are not making an arbitrary adjustment to certain structural equations; we are being guided by recently observed values of calculated residuals. In the absence of any particular measure, we shall always adjust the equation, positively or negatively, by the amount of the most recently observed residual, provided the external information indicates an adjustment in the same direction as these observed residuals.

The problem of detection of bias from the pattern of recent residuals is intimately connected with the problem of structural change. A pattern of several residuals of the same sign and similar magnitude may actually reflect a changed parameter. In this case the bias is more permanent and, in place of temporary corrections for nonzero values of disturbances, we must search for more permanent alterations of parameters. In some cases, we have adjusted disturbance values, on the basis of observed residuals, for reasons of expediency in particular forecasts required on short notice but after more careful and thoughtful research have basically modified parameters of the structural equations. One way of doing this is by the addition of new variables to the equation. Other changes have also been considered.

EXTRAPOLATIONS OF THE MODEL TO 1951 AND 1952

The estimated model presented above was based on a sample period with the latest observations including 1950. By early 1953, we were ready to experiment with the model, and observations were then available for 1951 and 1952; hence extrapolations to these latter two years are of the *ex-post* type. Our calculations were made in the first months of 1953 when the estimates of values for 1951 and 1952 were fairly well established, but the estimates have since been revised. In view of the difficulty of the calculations, we have not recomputed the extrapolations on the basis of the latest revisions of the figures. The observation values of predetermined and endogenous variables are internally consistent although they are not the same as currently available revised estimates. Revisions are not major, and principal conclusions to be drawn are firmly established although more refined calculations could be made. [1])

Two special points must be made clear in connection with *ex-post* extrapolations. In the first place, we treat various deflated or "real" magnitudes as exogenous exactly as we have done this in the sample period. Our procedure is different in true forecasting for the future, as explained above on pp. 36–40. For example, government expenditures in constant prices, G, is treated as exogenous in the present extrapolations. In true forecasting, only the *current dollar* value, and not the *constant dollar* value is treated as exogenous. A similar treatment is accorded taxes. For these variables we also do something different in true forecasting by assuming their *relation* to endogenous variables to be exogenous instead of assuming fixed amounts to be exogenous.

The second special point is that equations (12)–(15), referring to the money market, are not used in the extrapolations one year into the future. This was noted previously on p. 40, above. Since the only variables concerning interest and money that enter into the other equations are $(L_1)_{-1}$ and $(L_2)_{-1}$ we need not use equations (12)–(15). The lagged nature of these two variables makes them predetermined. In forecasting ahead for two or more periods, there would be a need for the money equations since unknown values of L_1 and L_2 would have to be used in the computations later than one year in advance. [2])

In the tables below, we present values of predetermined variables used in the extrapolations and their values for 1950. The latter serves to give the reader an idea of the changes occurring in the economy between the extrapolation period and the last sample year. The extrapolations are then presented together with observed values of endogenous variables for the period 1950–52. Two types of extrapolation are made. The first set gives the solution for endogenous variables under the assumption that all disturbances are zero. The second uses the assumption that the error of extrapolation will be the same as the error in the previous year.

---

[1]) The revisions mentioned in the text precede the more recent basic revisions announced in the summer of 1954.

[2]) See pp. 112–14 below.

TABLE I. *Predetermined Variables 1950–52*

Variable	1950	1951	1952
W_2	12.8	15.3	17.0
T_W	2.3	7.1	8.3
T_P	11.6	15.0	15.0
T_A	0.37	0.33	0.40
$(L_1)_{-1}$	98.5	99.4	94.5
N_P	151.7	154.4	157.0
C_{-1}	102.9	108.7	108.4
$(P+A+D-T_P-T_A)_{-1}$	45.75	46.35	47.35
K_{-1}	15.7	24.6	34.9
$(L_2)_{-1}$	36.8	37.7	37.8
T_C	10.1	12.3	11.7
B_{-1}	−5.6	−3.3	−1.9
$(P_C-T_C-S_P)_{-1}$	4.2	5.0	4.6
T	12.3	13.7	12.9
$(Y+T+D-W_2)_{-1}$	131.3	141.5	152.0
N	64.7	66.0	66.7
N_G	7.8	9.3	10.2
N_F	4.4	4.1	4.0
N_E	6.2	6.3	5.7
h	1.054	1.063	1.057
t	21	22	23
w_{-1}	274.5	287.1	309.9
$p_{-1}-p_{-2}$	−1.3	3.9	13.6
$(F_I)_{-1}$	3.7	4.8	4.2
p_I	196.5	245.4	231.6
G	18.5	26.6	32.8
F_E	7.1	8.5	8.5
F_A	155	184	163
$(W_1+W_2+P-S_P-T_W-T_P)_{-1}$	95.4	102.4	104.3

Note: Variables with a subscript −1 in this table are lagged variables, and the entries for them are the actual observations for the years 1949–51.

In Table II, the estimates of the form x_t^e are the solution values of the system under the assumption that all disturbances are zero. The alternative set of the form $x_{t-1} + (x_t^e - x_{t-1}^e)$ are adjusted solution values under the assumption that the same error will be made in extrapolating to the year t as was made in the year $t - 1$. If the last year of the sample period were $t - 1$, we should not interpret x_{t-1}^e

$$x_t = \text{actual value in year } t$$
$$x_t^e = \text{value estimated by model in year } t$$

	1950	1951			1952		
	x_{50}	x_{51}	x_{51}^e	$x_{50}+(x_{51}^e-x_{50}^e)$	x_{52}	x_{52}^e	$x_{51}+(x_{52}^e-x_{51}^e)$
C	108.7	108.4	108.7	112.7	110.2	113.0	112.7
P	34.9	37.0	33.6	37.2	35.5	35.7	39.1
D	15.9	17.7	15.3	17.0	20.6	16.6	19.0
S_P	2.28	1.43	−1.04	1.55	2.30	0.92	3.39
I	24.8	28.0	20.2	24.2	23.8	19.5	27.3
P_C	17.4	18.2	15.6	19.1	17.8	17.1	19.7
W_1	70.9	75.6	72.7	76.1	77.2	77.3	80.2
N_W	50.7	54.3	53.6	55.1	55.2	57.7	58.4
w	287.1	309.9	304.1	305.4	326.2	334.9	340.7
F_I	4.8	4.2	4.0	5.0	4.6	4.0	4.2
$Y+T+D$	154.3	167.3	159.9	166.9	170.8	169.9	177.3
Y	126.1	135.9	130.9	136.1	137.4	140.3	145.3
p	183.2	196.8	196.8	195.6	202.0	216.6	216.6
A	7.52	7.98	9.29	7.54	7.70	10.3	9.00

as an extrapolation; it is simply an estimated value. In making these adjustments for our nonlinear system, we fail to preserve certain identities among variables. It should also be pointed out that although there are 14 endogenous variables listed in Table II, only 10 are mutually independent. For the solution of the system, 4 identities are used together with 10 other structural equations. Since some variables can be derived from each other in these identities, there are essentially only 10 extrapolations.

In 1951, there appears to be a decided advantage in adjusting the solution values, but this advantage does not persist in 1952. For key variables like gross national product $(Y + T + D)$, our adjusted extrapolation is quite close in 1951 while the unadjusted extrapolation is quite close in 1952. For a variable like depreciation, D, we know that it follows a rather smooth path and does not have a large effect on the system for small fluctuations. We could easily make an adjustment in the estimation of this variable to improve the accuracy of its extrapolation without having much effect on the other estimates.

We have not made actual calculations with selective adjustments such as this for extrapolations to 1951 and 1952. However, on the basis of these findings we have used a selective process of assigning nonzero values to disturbances in *ex-ante* forecasting for 1953. These will be explained below.

Our main conclusion from the results of these extrapolations is that we have a system that gives a reasonably good interpretation of the workings of the economy in that it estimates the value of gross national product outside the sample observations by an error not exceeding 5 percent, whether we use one method of extrapolation or the other.

FORECASTS FOR 1953

On the basis of the empirical results for extrapolation to 1951 and 1952, we have experimented with *ex-ante* forecasting. We have made point forecasts of endogenous variables for the calendar year from our best information at the beginning of the year on the unlagged exogenous variables. 1953, as will be recalled, was the first year of a new political administration in the United States; hence, many basic policies were not clearly formulated at the time the forecast was prepared. We consequently made alternative forecasts of the behavior of the system under various different fiscal policies of the federal government. If our main conclusion drawn from the extrapolations to 1951 and 1952 is correct, we have a workable statistical model of the functioning of the economy, and one of the most significant uses of such a model is to examine the possible effects of different hypothetical policies. We may be able to make more accurate judgments about the effects of alternative policies than about pure prognosis of the actual course of economic activity.

It was not possible to embark on this phase of the research until February, 1953; therefore, we were making *ex-ante* forecasts for 1953 after approximately two months had elapsed. We had few statistical series available for January and February 1953 at that time, but we were obviously conscious, in a general way, of the economic environment.

Among the alternative assumptions considered, the basic situation, from which we begin the analysis, was that of continuation of the

82

existing tax system and the adoption of the budget recommended by the outgoing political administration. In Table III numerical values of predetermined variables used in this forecast are explicitly presented.

TABLE III. *Predetermined Variables, 1953 Forecast*

W_2	$\dfrac{37.2}{p10^{-2}}$	N_F	3.9
$(L_1)_{-1}$	95.8	N_E	5.7
N_P	159.2	h	1.057
C_{-1}	110.2	t	24
$(P+A+D-T_P-T_A)_{-1}$	48.4	w_{-1}	326.2
K_{-1}	38.1	$p_{-1}-p_{-2}$	5.2
$(L_2)_{-1}$	37.6	$(F_I)_{-1}$	4.6
B_{-1}	0.4	p_I	225
$(P_C-T_C-S_P)_{-1}$	3.8	G	$\dfrac{82.0}{p_G10^{-2}}$
$(Y+T+D-W_2)_{-1}$	153.9	F_E	$\dfrac{17.9}{p_E10^{-2}}$
N	67.35	F_A	138
N_G	10.4	$(W_1+W_2+P-S_P-T_W-T_P)_{-1}$	104.1

From observed data in 1951 and 1952, the following auxiliary equations were used for taxes and some prices:

$$T = 0.1185(Y + T + D) - \frac{1235.6}{p}$$

$$T_W = 0.24(W_1 + W_2) - \frac{2890.2}{p}$$

$$T_P = 0.2593P + \frac{1293.3}{p}$$

$$T_C = 0.685P_C + \frac{166.2}{p}$$

$$T_A = \frac{0.75}{p10^{-2}}; \quad \frac{p_G}{p} = 1.098; \quad \frac{p_E}{p} = 1.033$$

We shall call this set of assumptions variant I. The alternatives were constructed by changing the tax-expenditure assumptions of variant I.

TABLE IV. *Alternative Tax-Expenditure Assumptions, 1953 Forecasts*

Variant	Taxes	Expenditure
II	Same as variant I	Federal payrolls cut 5 percent
III	Corporation excess profits tax allowed to lapse July 1, 1953; continuation of remainder of tax system	Same as variant I
IV	Corporation excess profits tax allowed to lapse July 1, 1953; continuation of remainder of tax system	Federal payrolls cut 5 percent
V	Corporation excess profits tax allowed to lapse July 1, 1953; federal personal income taxes cut 5 percent; continuation of remainder of tax system	Same as variant I
VI	Corporation excess profits tax allowed to lapse July 1, 1953; federal personal income taxes cut 5 percent; continuation of remainder of tax system.	Federal payrolls cut 5 percent

Most of the discussion of policy at the time of forecast preparation was concerned with federal government decisions for the new fiscal year beginning July 1, 1953. We allowed for possible 10 percent reductions in personal income taxes and expenditures by treating them as 5 percent cuts for the calendar year. Tax reductions were introduced by changing the appropriate auxiliary functions. A cut in expenditures realized by cutting payrolls entailed simultaneous reductions in G, W_2, and N_G.

Point forecasts, assuming all disturbances to be zero, for each of the six variants are shown in Table V.

As we shall see from the *next* set of calculations and other data, there were strong reasons in early 1953 to believe that some of our equations were biased by calculable amounts; hence, the figures in Table V were not considered reliable forecasts of the level of activity

Variable	Variant					
	I	II	III	IV	V	VI
C	113.2	112.3	113.2	112.3	114.1	112.9
P	34.2	34.3	34.2	34.3	34.7	34.3
D	17.1	17.1	17.1	17.1	17.1	17.1
S_P	0.15	0.16	0.73	0.74	0.83	0.75
I	19.8	19.8	19.8	19.8	19.8	19.8
P_C	16.1	16.1	16.1	16.1	16.4	16.1
W_1	78.0	77.7	78.0	77.8	78.7	77.9
N_W	57.4	56.6	57.4	56.6	58.1	56.8
w	346.3	345.6	346.3	345.7	346.8	345.8
F_I	4.2	4.1	4.2	4.1	4.2	4.2
$Y+T+D$	170.4	168.1	170.4	168.2	171.9	168.7
Y	138.7	136.7	138.7	136.7	140.0	137.2
p	221.6	221.9	221.6	222.0	223.6	222.6
A	9.6	9.3	9.7	9.3	10.0	9.6

in 1953. Since it is thought that the main biases could readily be eliminated by correcting some equations for level, a major value of the results in Table V is to show the *sensitivity* of the system to various alternative lines of policy. Essentially, we have computed *short-run multipliers* in this table showing the change in endogenous variables associated with given changes in exogenous variables or tax-transfer functions after taking all interrelationships of the system into account.

In the short-run, one year in this instance, multiplier effects are much lower than those commonly supposed to exist. Under the stated changes in expenditures and taxes, we find little variation in aggregate real activity. All solution values exhibit the workings of a prosperous economy with high employment. Gross national product falls only $ 2.3 billion in 1939 prices as government expenditures in the form of payrolls are cut by 5 percent in current prices (variants I and II). The multiplier is somewhat less than 2. It is interesting to observe that the main effect of eliminating corporate excess profits taxes is to increase corporate saving (variants I and III). Corporate profits before taxes are not affected. Profits after taxes are up by virtue of the tax cut, and the surplus goes largely into saving. Since investment is lagged behind profits, perhaps too much in our model, tax savings do not affect current investment. In a longer-run analysis there would be multiplier effects as a result of increased investment.

The most deflationary variant is II (reduction of expenditures, taxes unchanged), and the most inflationary variant is V (reduction of taxes, expenditure unchanged). The extremes of real output are noticed in these two variants, as should be the case. II is the lowest and V is the highest. If expenditures and taxes are both reduced, output falls (variants I and VI).

In making our actual forecast for 1953, we first examined residuals, 1948–52, from each of the ten structural equations used in the solutions.

TABLE VI. *Residuals from Ten Structural Equations, 1948–52*

	Consumption equation	Investment equation	Corporate savings equation	Relation of corporate profits to nonwage non-farm income
	(1)	(2)	(3)	(4)
1948	−1.07	3.4	0.52	0.61
1949	0.56	−3.8	0.48	0.54
1950	0.51	4.0	−0.37	0.86
1951	−1.95	7.8	0.23	0.16
1952	−0.95	4.3	0.80	0.83

	Depreciation equation	Labor demand equation	Production function	Wage adjustment equation
	(5)	(6)	(7)	(8)
1948	1.12	0.50	−1.88	0.37
1949	1.04	−0.54	−0.71	−8.08
1950	1.57	0.72	3.53	0.17
1951	2.02	0.18	5.53	5.33
1952	3.96	−0.49	7.15	−6.78

	Import demand equation	Farm income equation
	(9)	(10)
1948	−0.23	1.04
1949	−0.15	−1.84
1950	0.93	−2.82
1951	0.19	−2.13
1952	0.66	−2.11

In three equations [(4), (5), and (10)] we are consistently incorrect in the same direction for the last four sample years. Because of some technical problems in the revaluation of depreciation we felt most certain about the persistence of bias in equation (5). We were, however, able to eliminate this problem in a later version of this model, as will be explained below. Equations (4) and (10) are not entirely satisfactory as structural estimates in any case. Revision of them for bias has relatively small effect on our estimates of general activity levels. Their main effect is on the *distribution* of income among farmers, corporations, and other nonwage earners of our society.

The production function could be underestimating output, as it appears to do in the last three years, either because technology is increasing at a rate more rapid than our linear trend or because our measures of capital lack adequacy. The investment equation shows a similar tendency to underestimate activity in the last three years. Independent statistical estimates of capital formation obtained from surveys of business investment intentions led us to believe that our error in this equation would persist into 1953. A correction for the level of investment activity is the most important in affecting the forecasted level of output. We had strong outside information to use in adjusting this equation. None of the other equations showed equally persistent biases in the form of residuals of similar algebraic magnitude. None showed runs of the last three consecutive observations except (9) [1]. The most important remaining equation admitting of possible adjustment is the consumption equation, but we made no change here because consumer surveys of buying plans showed large prospective outlays, especially in the durables field, for 1953. We could not reconcile this information with a tendency to overestimate consumption in 1951 and 1952.

We added, algebraically, the 1952 residuals of equations (2), (4), (5), (7) and (10) to the structural estimates of the constant term in each. We then solved the resulting adjusted set for the endogenous

---

[1] A computing error led us to attribute a negative instead of a positive residual to this equation in 1950; hence we made no adjustment to it in forecasting. We know, however, that small changes in this particular equation will have negligible effect on the solution to the whole system.

variables under variant III, our best judgment, at the time, of the government tax-expenditure policy.

TABLE VII. *Forecasts for 1953*

C	114.4	P_C	17.5	$Y+T+D$	177.4
P	35.1	W_1	80.4	Y	141.1
D	21.0	N_W	57.1	p	213.7
S_P	1.13	w	346.1	A	8.3
I	24.2	F_I	4.1		

This forecast anticipated a growth in real activity and employment. Continued upward pressure on money wage rates was expected, as was more price inflation. Agricultural income was forecasted at a lower level than in 1952. In retrospect this appears to have been an excellent forecast, its main error being an overestimate of price inflation. A major policy change assumed in making this forecast was the abolition of corporate excess profits taxes after July 1, 1953. Political developments did not bring this about, but we may point to the results of Table V to indicate that this assumption has little effect on any forecast values other than corporate savings.

It is worth pointing out that this forecast went against much of the prevailing "expert" opinion. Several economists and business forecasters expected a significant downturn after the middle of 1953, and did not anticipate yearly totals as much above those of 1952 as indicated by our Table VII, nor as actually occurred. Although there was a downturn in the second half of 1953, the economy registered substantial growth for the year as a whole.

VI. REVISION OF THE MODEL AND FORECASTS FOR 1954

As an example of the laborious, but necessary, steps in a well-functioning program of econometric research and application we show the revision of the model to bring it up to date during 1953, in preparation for forecasts in 1954.

Estimates from relatively small samples, such as the 20–25 annual observations frequently used in econometric model construction, will sometimes be sensitive to small changes in observed data. Economic time series are constantly being revised by the primary data-processing agencies, and new observations are continuously accumulating. The best practice in forecasting from econometric models is to recalculate all parameter estimates from the latest revised set of data. For example, in order to make forecasts for 1954, we revised all estimates of our equation system, based on sample data 1929–41 and 1946–52, thus including two years' observations beyond the sample used for equations (1)–(15) on pp. 51–53 above. Naturally, the latest revisions of data were used in the reestimation of the model.

Three refinements were introduced prior to recalculation, and these have a slight influence on changes noted in selected equations. Imports were redefined to include only sales to persons and businesses in the United States. Formerly we calculated our import variable as total purchases in the United States less direct estimates of unilateral transfers overseas by the United States government.

The variable representing farm income, A, in the above model was changed by splitting it into two components A_1 and A_2. A_1 excludes government payments to farmers, while A_2 consists wholly of government payments to farmers. Thus we have the identity

$$A = A_1 + A_2.$$

Furthermore, the agricultural income equation was designed in the later model to "explain" only A_1, the endogenous component of A.

89

A_2 is an exogenous variable. This equation was also changed by deflating nonagricultural disposable income by the price of agricultural output, p_A, instead of by the price of total output, p. This modification necessitated the use of an additional equation to account for the relation between farm and nonfarm prices.

The third refinement was to add a variable to the depreciation equation. Formerly, we had a simple technical relation making depreciation a linear function of the stock of capital. At the postwar levels of high activity, we found that this equation consistently underestimated depreciation; hence we included the value of private gross national product in constant prices as an additional variable to show the influence of intensity of use on depreciation of capital. In a statistical sense, this change appears to lend improvement to the depreciation equation.

Other modifications were considered and given experimental treatment in the calculations, but none of them appear to be fruitful. As before, we experimented with investment equations in which current nonwage income and long term interest rates were also used as variables, but none of the estimates were at all reasonable. In the empirical equation relating corporate profits to nonwage nonfarm income we experimented with lagged values of nonwage nonfarm income, but found the results to be obscured by multicollinearity.

Using the same estimation procedures as in the previous model, practically the same set of predetermined variables for the computation of the limited information estimates, and the same notation (except for the changes noted in the preceding paragraphs), we estimated

$$(1)* \quad C_t = -22.26 + 0.55(W_1 + W_2 - T_W)_t + 0.41(P - T_P - S_P)_t +$$
$$\quad (9.66) \ (0.06) \qquad\qquad\qquad (0.05)$$
$$\quad + 0.34(A_1 + A_2 - T_A)_t + 0.26C_{t-1} + 0.072(L_1)_{t-1} + 0.26(N_P)_t$$
$$\quad (0.04) \qquad\qquad (0.075) \quad (0.025) \qquad (0.10)$$
$$\delta^2/S^2 = 1.98$$

$$(2)* \quad I_t = -16.71 + 0.78(P - T_P + A_1 + A_2 - T_A + D)_{t-1} - 0.073K_{t-1} +$$
$$\quad (4.74) \ (0.18) \qquad\qquad\qquad\qquad\qquad (0.067)$$
$$\quad + 0.14(L_2)_{t-1}$$
$$\quad (0.11)$$
$$\delta^2/S^2 = 2.08$$

(3)* $(S_P)_t = -3.53 + 0.72(P_C - T_C)_t + 0.076(P_C - T_C - S_P)_{t-1} -$
    (1.02) (0.06)   (0.254)

$$- 0.028 B_{t-1}$$
$$(0.019)$$

$$\delta^2/S^2 = 0.99$$

(4)* $(P_C)_t = -7.60 + 0.68 P_t$
    (0.54) (0.02)

$$\delta^2/S^2 = 1.28$$

(5)* $D_t = 7.25 + 0.10 \dfrac{K_t + K_{t-1}}{2} + 0.044(Y + T + D - W_2)_t$
    (0.80) (0.01)   (0.008)

$$\delta^2/S^2 = 0.94$$

(6)* $(W_1)_t = -1.40 + 0.24(Y + T + D - W_2)_t +$
    (1.46) (0.07)

$$+ 0.24(Y + T + D - W_2)_{t-1} + 0.29t$$
$$(0.06) \qquad\qquad\qquad (0.125)$$

$$\delta^2/S^2 = 2.45$$

(7)* $(Y + T + D - W_2)_t = -26.08 + 2.17[h(N_W - N_G) + N_E + N_F]_t +$
    (7.27) (0.18)

$$+ 0.16 \dfrac{K_t + K_{t-1}}{2} + 2.05t$$
$$(0.05) \qquad\qquad (0.16)$$

$$\delta^2/S^2 = 1.09$$

(8)* $w_t - w_{t-1} = 4.11 - 0.74(N - N_W - N_E - N_F)_t +$
    (4.85) (0.61)

$$+ 0.52(p_{t-1} - p_{t-2}) + 0.54t$$
$$(0.28) \qquad\qquad (0.24)$$

$$\delta^2/S^2 = 2.38$$

(9)* $(F_I)_t = 0.32 +$
    (0.49)

$$+ 0.0060(W_1 + W_2 - T_W + P - T_P + A_1 + A_2 - T_A)_t \frac{p_t}{(p_I)_t} + 0.81(F_I)_{t-1}$$
$$(0.0084) \qquad\qquad\qquad\qquad\qquad\qquad\qquad\qquad\qquad (0.21)$$

$$\delta^2/S^2 = 2.33$$

$$(10)^* \ (A_1)_t \frac{p_t}{(p_A)_t} = -0.36 + 0.054(W_1 + W_2 - T_W + P - T_P - S_P)_t \frac{p_t}{(p_A)_t}$$
$$(2.12) \ (0.045)$$

$$-0.007(W_1 + W_2 - T_W + P - T_P - S_P)_{t-1} \frac{p_{t-1}}{(p_A)_{t-1}} + 0.012(F_A)_t$$
$$(0.043) \qquad\qquad\qquad (0.006)$$

$$\delta^2/S^2 = 0.85$$

$$(11)^* \ (p_A)_t = -131.17 + 2.32 p_t$$
$$(15.3) \quad (0.11)$$

$$\delta^2/S^2 = 0.74$$

$$(12)^* \ (L_1)_t = 0.14(W_1 + W_2 - T_W + P - T_P - S_P + A_1 + A_2 - T_A)_t +$$
$$+ 76.03(i_L - 2.0)_t^{\ -0.84 \atop (0.03)}$$
$$(15.31)$$

$$\delta^2/S^2 = 0.73 \text{ (for the logarithmic form of residuals)}$$

$$(13)^* \ (L_2)_t = -0.34 + 0.26(W_1)_t - 1.02(i_S)_t - 0.26(p_t - p_{t-1}) + 0.61(L_2)_{t-1}$$
$$(0.99) \ (0.03) \qquad (0.19) \qquad (0.06) \qquad\qquad (0.06)$$

$$\delta^2/S^2 = 1.72$$

$$(14)^* \ i_L = 2.58 + 0.44(i_S)_{t-3} + 0.26(i_S)_{t-5}$$
$$(0.15) \quad (0.10) \qquad\quad (0.09)$$

$$\delta^2/S^2 = 0.84$$

$$(15)^* \ 100 \frac{(i_S)_t - (i_S)_{t-1}}{(i_S)_{t-1}} = 11.17 - 0.67 R_t$$
$$(7.81) \quad (0.30)$$

$$\delta^2/S^2 = 1.59$$

$$C_t + I_t + G_t + (F_E)_t - (F_I)_t = Y_t + T_t + D_t$$

$$(W_1)_t + (W_2)_t + P_t + (A_1)_t + (A_2)_t = Y_t$$

$$h_t \frac{w_t}{p_t} (N_W)_t = (W_1)_t + (W_2)_t$$

$$K_t - K_{t-1} = I_t - D_t$$

$$B_t - B_{t-1} = (S_P)_t$$

In Figures 21–30 the estimated equations are plotted for each of the sample years.

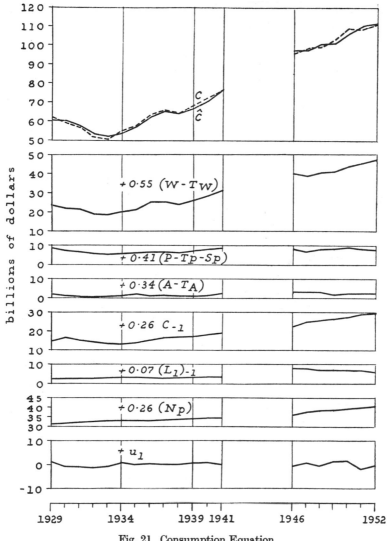

Fig. 21. Consumption Equation

The majority of differences in parameter estimates obtained from the revised and augmented sample are not large and can be accounted for by the presence of sampling error. In the corporate savings equation, the coefficient of past dividends changes from negative in (3) to

93

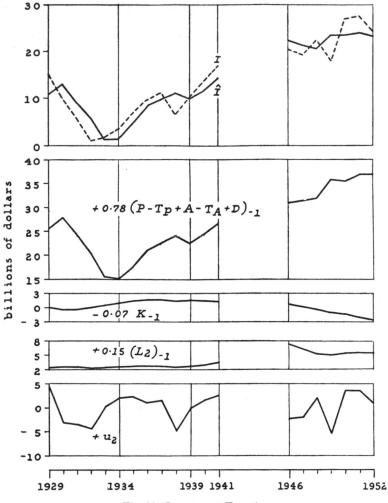

Fig. 22. Investment Equation

positive in (3*). Both have wide sampling error. They are not significantly different from zero; hence the change in sign is understandable, and we are not led to exclude this variable on the basis of the new computations. The coefficients of liquid assets in the consumption function and of capital in the production function both increase in absolute value and relative to their estimated sampling errors.

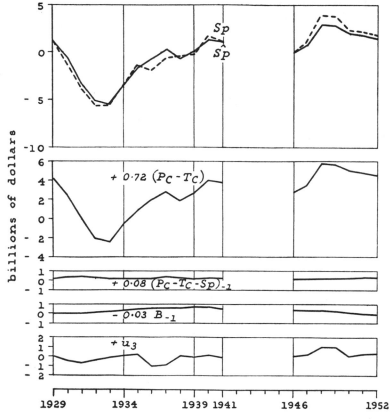

Fig. 23. Corporate Savings Equation

The reverse happens to the coefficient of capital in the investment equation. The import demand equation and the agricultural income determination equation both undergo substantial change as a result of different definitions of variables used. Neither of these two equations is satisfactory in the present or old formulation, and steps must be taken to improve both estimates by decomposition of the aggregative relations into more detailed subgroups.

FORECASTS FOR 1954

The model, recomputed through 1952, was used for forecasts into 1954. These forecasts were prepared in December 1953 using estimates

95

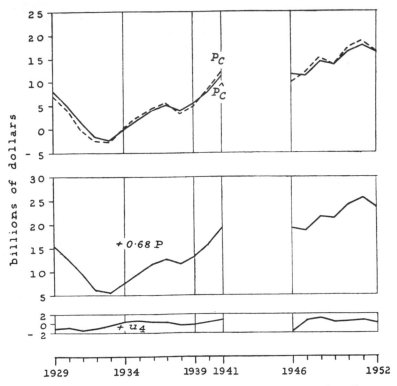

Fig. 24. Relation between Corporate Profits and Nonwage Nonfarm Income

for 1953 as lags in the forecast solution. This is an example of true advance forecasting which contains the serious complication that we are less certain than at a later time about the values of predetermined variables, whether they be lags or exogenous magnitudes.

The fiscal situation was somewhat different at the end of 1953 as compared with a year earlier, but there was still some uncertainty about the precise tax functions or government expenditure amounts to be used in forecasting; therefore we prepared, as previously, alternative fiscal policies and the associated forecasts from them. The preferred forecast we shall call variant I. It assumed statutory reduction of personal income taxes on January 1, 1954, (approximately 10 percent), statutory removal of the excess profits tax on January 1, 1954, and a rewriting of tax laws during the year leading to a further

96

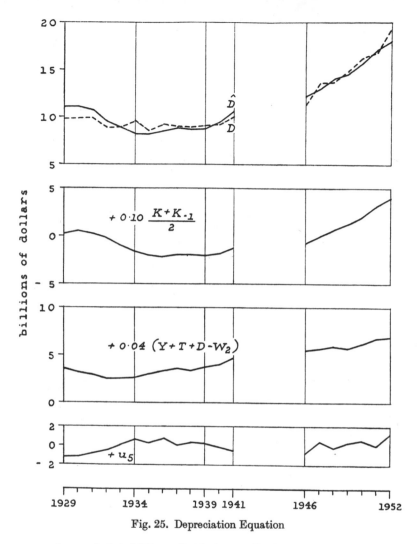

Fig. 25. Depreciation Equation

revenue loss of $ 1 billion divided equally between personal and corporate income taxes. [1]) According to our concept of measuring

---

[1]) The assumed reductions in personal income taxes and removal of the excess profits taxes are parallel to assumptions made about these two tax components in forecasts for 1953. In that situation, however, tax changes were assumed to be applicable to only one-half the calendar year.

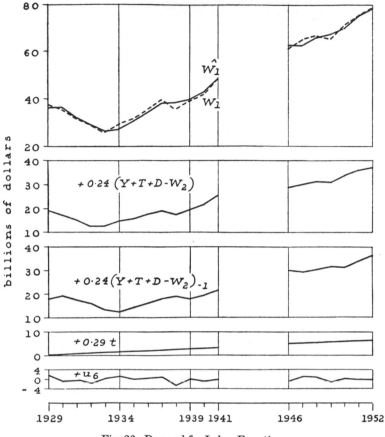

Fig. 26. Demand for Labor Equation

government expenditures on goods and services, we assumed a cut of $ 1.2 billion under this variant. This net amount consists of a deeper cut in federal expenditures offset by a trend rise in state and local government expenditures. Together with the net cut in government expenditures, we have a decline in the number of government employees and the public wage bill. The estimated predetermined variables used in making the preferred forecast for 1954 are given in Table VIII. We also present values for 1952 and estimates for 1953 in order that the reader can make comparisons. These may differ from comparable items in Table I because of data revisions.

98

TABLE VIII. *Predetermined Variables, 1954 Forecasts*

	1952	1953 (estimates)	1954 (estimates)
W_2	$\dfrac{34.0}{p10^{-2}}$	$\dfrac{35.16}{p10^{-2}}$	$\dfrac{34.6}{p10^{-2}}$
C_{-1}	108.5	111.4	116.1
$(L_1)_{-1}$	93.3	95.2	99.7
N_P	157.0	159.7	162.4
$(P-T_P+A_1+A_2-T_A+D)_{-1}$	47.6	47.8	47.6
K_{-1}	36.6	41.5	45.8
$(L_2)_{-1}$	37.9	38.1	38.8
$(P_C-T_C-S_P)_{-1}$	4.6	4.5	4.6
B_{-1}	-1.71	0.19	1.11
$(Y+T+D-W_2)_{-1}$	151.8	155.2	162.9
t	23	24	25
h	1.057	1.049	1.04
N_G	10.4	10.5	10.2
N_F	4.0	3.7	3.5
N_E	6.3	6.5	6.6
w_{-1}	309.9	326.2	349.7
N	66.6	66.9	67.4
$p_{-1}-p_{-2}$	13.9	4.9	2.0
$(F_I)_{-1}$	5.2	5.5	6.2
p_I	252	241	241
$\left[(W_1+W_2-T_W+P-T_P-S_P)\dfrac{p}{p_A}\right]_{-1}$	64.7	71.0	84.3
F_A	164	131	131
G	$\dfrac{74.1}{p_G10^{-2}}$	$\dfrac{79.8}{p_G10^{-2}}$	$\dfrac{78.6}{p_G10^{-2}}$
F_E	$\dfrac{17.1}{p_E10^{-2}}$	$\dfrac{16.2^*}{p_E10^{-2}}$	$\dfrac{18.5}{p_E10^{-2}}$
p_A	303	272	269
A_2	$\dfrac{0.3}{p10^{-2}}$	$\dfrac{0.3}{p10^{-2}}$	$\dfrac{0.3}{p10^{-2}}$

* 16.2 is a residual estimate derived from independent estimates of the nte foreign balance and imports. Our best direct estimate is 17.8.

$$T = 0.0924(Y+T+D) - \frac{275.4}{p}$$

$$T_W = 0.1549W_1 + 0.1310W_2 - \frac{1398.1}{p}$$

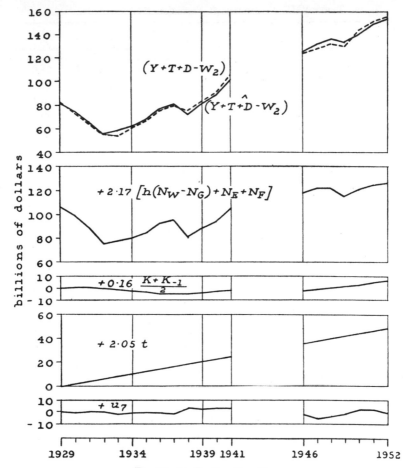

Fig. 27. Production Function

$$T_C = 0.4497 P_C + \frac{548.2}{p}$$

$$T_P = 0.248(P - T_C - S_P) + 0.2695 \frac{p_{-1}}{p}(P - T_C - S_P)_{-1} +$$

$$+ 0.4497 P_C - \frac{1162.1}{p}$$

100

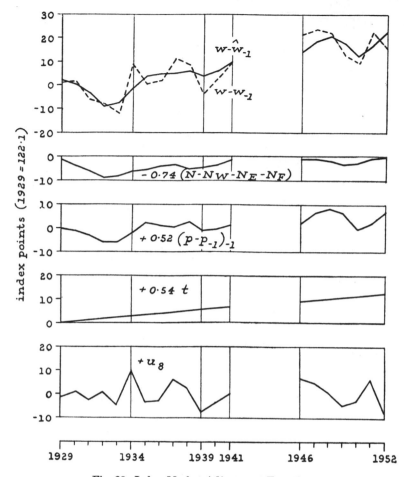

Fig. 28. Labor Market Adjustment Equation

$$T_A = \frac{50.0}{p}$$

$$\frac{p_G}{p} = 1.093 \qquad\qquad \frac{p_E}{p} = 1.018$$

These tax-transfer equations have a slightly different form from those used in the 1953 forecasts. These differences are in addition to those occasioned by the fact that our assumed tax laws are changed from

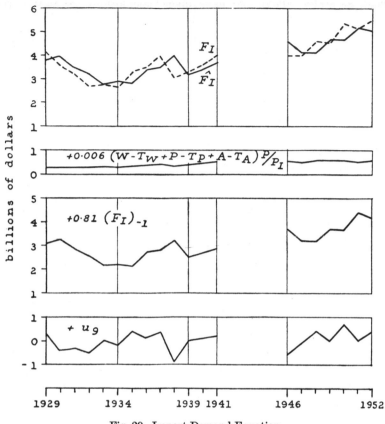

Fig. 29. Import Demand Equation

1953 to 1954. We have estimated some components of each of the tax-transfer variables as direct constants for 1954 where we have good evidence of insensitivity to the level of activity. The function for T_P is not estimated directly from observations on T_P and P. First, a relation is established between T_C and P_C. Then we estimate a relation between $T_P - T_C$ and $P - T_C - S_P$. These variables both refer to nonwage, nonfarm, noncorporate data. The equation for T_P is finally obtained as the sum of those for T_C and $T_P - T_C$. In the latter of these two, the payment of taxes out of income is partly lagged and partly current according to present methods of collection.

In addition to the assumptions connected with the preferred fore cast, as stated above, we have made calculations for four variants listed in Table IX.

TABLE IX. *Alternative Tax-Expenditure Assumptions, 1954 Forecasts*

Variant	Taxes	Expenditures
II	Same as variant I except for the addition of statutory reduction of corporate profits tax and selected excise taxes on April 1.	Federal government expenditures $ 5.05 billion greater than on variant I and federal payrolls $ 2.2 billion greater.
III	Same as variant I.	Federal government expenditures $ 5 billion greater than on variant I, and no change in government payrolls.
IV	Differs from variant I in that increased social security contributions of 1.0 percentage point are assumed to be in effect for the year and that excise taxes are assumed to *rise* by $ 1 billion. There is no revenue loss from rewriting of tax laws under this variant.	Federal government expenditures $ 2.95 billion lower than on variant I and federal payrolls $ 1.3 billion lower.
V	Differs from variant I on all tax items considered except corporate income tax. No cut in federal personal income tax, no cut in excess profits taxes, increase in social security contributions, increase in excise taxes of $ 1 billion, and no revenue loss through rewriting of tax laws.	Federal government expenditures $ 2.95 billion lower than on variant I and federal payrolls $ 1.3 billion lower.

Variants II and III are inflationary, II more so than III. Variants IV and V are deflationary, V more so than IV. Since variant III differs from I only by the amount of government expenditures without consequent changes induced in government payrolls, we can estimate

103

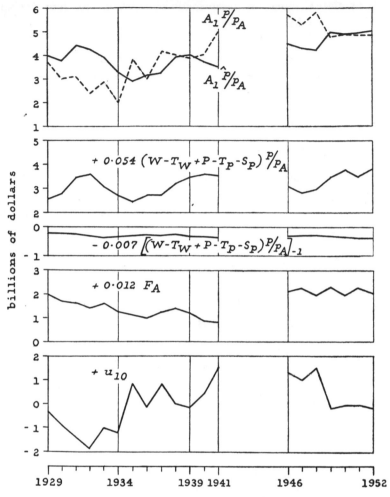

Fig. 30. Agricultural Income Determination Equation

a pure multiplier effect of expenditures by comparing the different levels of activity calculated for I and III. [1])

On the basis of our experience with the first model extrapolated to

[1]) The conventional multiplier concept may assume tax yield to be constant with expenditure alone varying. We assume, in our numerical computation, that the tax-transfer *function* remains invariant with expenditures changing.

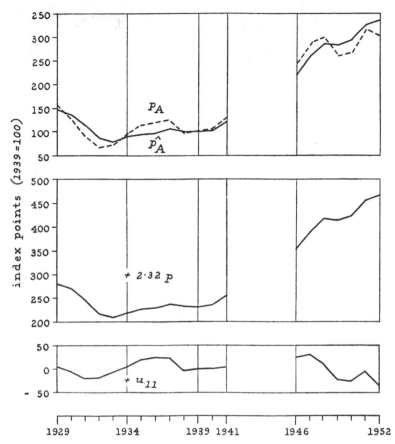

Fig. 31. Relation between Agricultural and Nonagricultural Prices

1951, 1952, and 1953, we found that it is better to correct equations selectively for persistent biases in residuals and independent outside information rather than assume either that all disturbances are zero or equal to the estimated value for the preceding year. We, therefore, computed residuals for all equations for the period 1948–52 in advance of forecasting. It was decided not to include estimates for 1953 at the time this analysis was first undertaken — in September 1953 — although a few such estimates had to be used as initial conditions in the actual forecasts.

TABLE X. *Residuals from Eleven Structural Equations, 1948–52*

	Consumption equation	Investment equation	Corporate savings equation	Relation of corporate profits to nonwage nonfarm income
	(1)*	(2)*	(3)*	(4)*
1948	−0.4	2.1	1.11	1.05
1949	1.4	−5.6	1.03	0.42
1950	1.7	3.5	0.10	0.56
1951	−1.9	3.6	0.32	0.86
1952	−0.4	1.1	0.43	0.28

	Depreciation equation	Labor demand equation	Production function	Wage adjustment equation
	(5)*	(6)*	(7)*	(8)*
1948	−0.26	0.74	−3.6	1.2
1949	0.23	−1.46	−1.3	−5.0
1950	0.53	0.68	2.2	−2.3
1951	−0.07	0.16	2.3	5.5
1952	1.30	0.35	1.0	−7.3

	Import demand equation	Farm income equation	Relation of agricultural to nonagricultural prices
	(9)*	(10)*	(11)*
1948	0.4	1.58	12
1949	−0.1	−0.25	−23
1950	0.7	0.03	−26
1951	0.0	−0.06	− 9
1952	0.4	−0.20	−35

The last set of residuals, that for (11)*, shows the most striking and persistent departure from our structural equations in recent years. We could see that use of (11)* in any forecast for 1954 would lead to serious bias since it is estimated from data in a sample period of parity legislation. The new farm policy of the federal administration since 1953, would lead to even larger departures from our estimated equation. Knowing that we wanted to forecast into a period of relaxed farm parity policy, we decided to suppress equation (11)* and use the current value (November 1953) for farm prices for the forecast

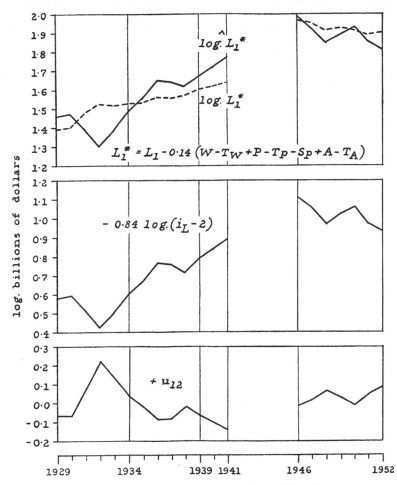

Fig. 32. Household Liquidity Preference Equation

period. This forecast is essentially that made by expert agricultural economists and superior to any produced by the use of (11)*.

The other residuals did not call for adjustment of respective equations. [1] In the investment equation, we had a succession of three

---

[1] In computations prior to the preparation of this volume, we committed a numerical error in the estimation of the constant term of (10)*. This error made the recent residuals look consistently positive; therefore we added the (incorrect) 1952 residual to (10)* in computing forecasts. It happened that this adjustment is practically the same thing as using the correct constant term and assuming a zero disturbance. This is not accidental.

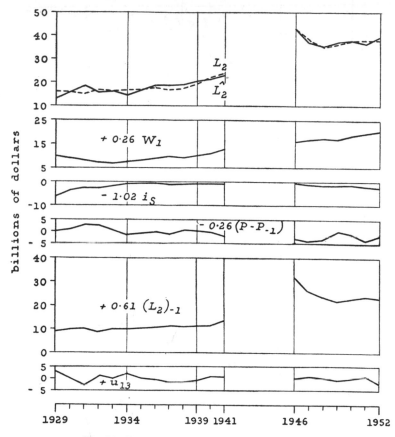

Fig. 33. Business Liquidity Preference Equation

positive residuals, but surveys of investment intentions indicated a slight drop for 1954, in contrast to expectations of increase for 1953; hence we assumed zero disturbance in equation (2)*. It is also to be noted that the residual for 1952 is relatively small in equation (2)*. In fact most of our equations in this group show a tendency toward small residuals by 1952, and we used this information in deciding not to adjust any other equations in advance of forecasting. Equations (3)* and (4)* were possible candidates, but they showed small residuals for 1952, and adjustment in these cases would have practically no effect on our results. The residuals in (6)* and (7)* were not considered

108

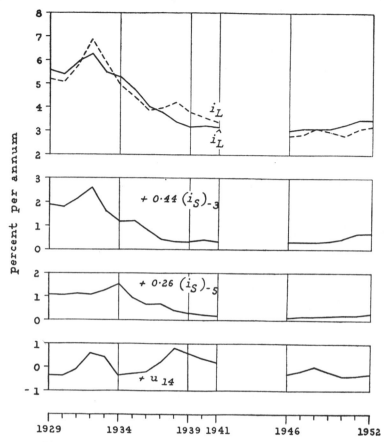

Fig. 34. Relation between Short and Long Term Interest Rates

to be sufficiently persistent or large to justify a choice other than zero. Consumer surveys made in September 1953 indicated relative optimism for the purchasing outlook, and we made no adjustment to (1)*.

In forecasting for 1953, our residuals (Table VI) were relatively larger or growing in the latest year for which reliable data were available. This was generally not the case in forecasting for 1954 (Table X); therefore we made fewer adjustments on the basis of examining the residuals and independent sample survey data.

Using the predetermined variables in Table VIII and the estimated tax-transfer equations, we solved our equation system for predictions

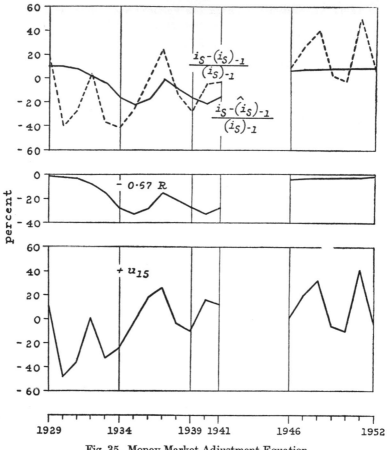

Fig. 35. Money Market Adjustment Equation

of endogenous variables in 1954. In each variant after I, we used appropriately adjusted values of government expenditures and tax parameters. The results are presented in Table XI.

Our optimal forecasts, variant I, show a slight drop in economic activity in 1954 compared with 1953. A continued upward pressure on wages is predicted. Since wages and other types of income are closely linked in our model by equation (6)* and the definition of national income, we find a simultaneous increase in price level. The 1953 forecast overestimated the increase in price level, although it was substantially correct on estimates of wages and real output;

TABLE XI. *Estimates of Endogenous Variables under Alternative Tax-Expenditure Assumptions, 1954*

Variable	Variant					Observations	
	I	II	III	IV	V	1953 (estimate from first 9 mos.)	1952
C	117.3	118.0	117.5	116.4	115.7	116.1	111.4
P	36.1	37.3	37.3	35.1	34.8	36.2	35.2
D	19.1	19.1	19.2	19.0	19.0	21.7	19.4
S_P	1.7	2.6	2.0	1.2	0.4	0.9	1.9
I	22.7	22.7	22.7	22.7	22.7	26.0	24.3
P_C	16.9	17.6	17.7	16.2	16.0	17.5	16.5
W_1	82.3	82.7	82.8	82.1	81.9	84.7	78.7
N_W	56.5	57.7*	57.3	55.4	55.2	56.8	56.0
w	367.8	368.7*	368.5	367.0	366.9	349.7	326.2
F_I	6.0	6.0	6.0	6.0	6.0	6.2	5.5
$Y+T+D$	174.8	177.2	176.5	173.3	172.8	180.1	172.0
Y	140.8	143.2	142.3	139.1	138.6	144.1	137.9
p	220.5	222.8	223.6	217.4	216.5	204.4	202.4
A_1	6.5	6.6	6.5	6.4	6.4	6.0	7.3

* If the index of hours worked is maintained at its 1953 level, as would be consistent with the more inflationary aspects of variant II, the only variables significantly affected are N_W an w. They become 57.2 and 368.4 respectively.

therefore we have reason to believe that the estimate of the price level is biased upward, although we do not have a satisfactory measure of the amount of bias.

Although we forecast only a slight downturn in economic activity, it is interesting to note that our model is able to pick out this turning point. Preliminary forecasts, made at the end of October 1953 when evidence of a downturn was otherwise scanty, were essentially the same as those in Table XI. As should be the case, real output and the price level are larger for more expansionary and smaller for more contractionary fiscal policies.

Analysis of alternative fiscal policies is often couched in terms of multiplier effects on gross national product. The most straightforward method of obtaining such multipliers in our complex system would be to derive the explicit algebraic solution for $Y + T + D$ in terms of predetermined variables. The one-year multiplier of a change in a

111

single exogenous variable (or parameter of a tax function) is then the partial derivative of $Y + T + D$ with respect to that variable. Equilibrium multipliers could similarly be derived from the explicit solution for $Y + T + D$ in terms of exogenous variables only. Although we have not yet computed either type of explicit solution, we may make some preliminary estimates of gross national product multipliers from the results presented in Table XI.

The difference in assumptions between variants I and III lies wholly in government expenditures, the tax functions being identical under the two variants. The difference in government expenditures of $ 1.6 billion in 1939 dollars generates a difference of $ 1.7 billion in gross national product. This is a short-run multiplier of about 1.0. At the higher activity levels of variant III, the same tax functions resulted in $ 0.8 billion more tax yields than with variant I. To get an idea of the multiplier of government expenditures with tax *yields* constant, we may compare variants I and II which differ by only $ 0.1 billion in total tax yields. The $ 1.8 billion difference in 1939 dollars in government expenditures generates a $ 2.4 billion difference in gross national product, indicating a multiplier of about 1.5.

Two-Year Multipliers

In analyzing fiscal policies which operate in a dynamic system where behavioral lags play a significant role, it is important to consider their effects over more than a single period. This might be done from an explicit solution of the model considered as a difference equation system, with each endogenous variable expressed in terms of exogenous variables and lagged values of itself and of no other endogenous variable. With initial conditions and time paths of exogenous variables specified, the time paths of the endogenous variables could be obtained. Different specifications would generate different time paths and thus provide a basis for comparing alternative policies.

We have not yet derived such an explicit solution; in lieu of this, after making our forecasts for 1954, we allowed variants I and III, which have the same tax functions, to run for two years by preparing alternative "forecasts" of 1955 activity. These were not intended as realistic forecasts; they were simply designed to provide an additional period for the operation of the alternative government expenditure programs. Several of the exogenous variables were held constant at their 1954 values; others (population, labor force) were extrapolated along smooth time trends.

The treatment we had given to liquid asset holdings in making single year forecasts – ignoring the money market equations and hence requiring L_1 and L_2 to appear only as predetermined variables – was not available to us in making forecasts for longer periods. The money market equations should be used to determine L_1 and L_2 as endogenous magnitudes for 1954 which appear as $(L_1)_{-1}$ and $(L_2)_{-1}$ in the non-money market equations for 1955 forecasts.

As we do with all our structural equations, we examined the residuals, for recent years, of the money market equations.

TABLE XII. *Residuals from Money Market Structural Equations, 1948–53*

	Household liquidity preference equation [1])	Business liquidity preference equation	Relation between short and long term interest rates	Money market adjustment equation
	(12)*	(13)*	(14)*	(15)*
1948	0.064	−0.07	−0.011	31.8
1949	0.030	−0.17	−0.168	− 5.3
1950	−0.017	0.20	−0.371	−10.0
1951	0.040	1.07	−0.349	41.1
1952	0.084	−1.47	−0.314	− 1.4
1953	0.174	−3.03	−0.158	0.9

The persistent underestimation in the long-term interest rate equation and the size of some of the recent residuals in the short-term interest rate equation led us to suppress equations (14)* and (15)* when we made "forecasts" for 1955. Instead we set the 1954 interest rates for both variants at their latest reported levels (October 1953): $i_L = 3.40$ and $i_S = 2.50$. Equation (12)* shows a tendency towards residuals of increasing size; in terms of dollars rather than logarithms, the 1953 calculated value of L_1 was \$ 72.0 billion dollars while its observed value was \$ 99.7 billion dollars. Therefore, we added the 1953 residual to the equation before using this equation. Equation (13)* was used without change.

---

[1]) For the logarithmic form of the equation.

With these modifications, our model was used to produce alternative "forecasts" of 1955 activity, under fiscal policy variants I and III. The result was that the $ 1.6 billion difference in government purchases generated a $ 2.6 billion difference in gross national product in the second year. The indicated two-year multiplier of government purchases, with tax functions constant, is about 1.6.

APPENDIX I. THE BASIC TIME SERIES

This appendix contains a detailed listing of the sources and methods used in deriving the basic time series in our model. First, however, we will sketch in general terms the manner in which some of our key series are derived from published material.

GENERAL COMMENTS

INCOME AND PRODUCT FLOWS

The National Income and Product Accounts of the United States Department of Commerce [1]) present a consistent picture of the national income and product flows in considerable detail. On the product side, our series are taken bodily from the Constant Dollar Gross National Product series, with one exception. In our import series government purchases from abroad (including unilateral transfers), are deducted from the USDC import series. In order to keep the GNP total unchanged, we deduct the same figure from Government Purchases of Goods and Services.

On the income side, constant dollar series have not been prepared by the USDC. We first construct our series in current dollars from the detailed USDC breakdowns and then use the Implicit Price Deflator of the Constant Dollar GNP series as a measure of the general price level to obtain deflated series for the income flows. An exception is made to this procedure: capital consumption allowances are deflated by an index of capital equipment prices. In order to maintain the income identity in *constant dollar* terms our deflated nonwage nonfarm income is obtained by 1) deflating, by the general price level, current dollar nonwage nonfarm income *before* the deduction of capital

---

[1]) Referred to in this appendix as the "National Accounts". The Nation:.: Accounts for 1929–1948 are in the *Survey of Current Business: 1951 National Income Supplement,* Parts IV and V; for 1949–1952 in *Survey of Current Business,* July 1953, pp. 6–32. The import and export components of Net Foreign Investment were obtained in private correspondence with the USDC.

consumption allowances, and then 2) deducting constant dollar capital consumption allowances.

Before doing this, we make a major adjustment of the USDC capital consumption allowances series to obtain concepts of net investment, profits, and national income more closely suited to our objectives. In the USDC series, capital services used are written off on the basis of the original cost of the capital equipment. In a period of changing prices, this fails to reflect the true value of the capital consumed. Therefore, we convert the USDC series to a replacement cost basis, valuing the capital consumed each period at the prices of that period; and then obtain the constant dollar series, D, by the use of the USDC Implicit Price Deflator of Gross Private Domestic Investment. Our measure of net investment is obtained by subtracting D from the constant dollar estimate of gross private domestic capital formation.

This adjustment of depreciation costs, of course, necessitates a corresponding adjustment of the USDC profit series. The adjusting item – the constant dollar excess of replacement cost over original cost depreciation – is allocated between corporate profits and entrepreneurial income. Corporate savings are similarly affected.

The currently published USDC National Accounts run back to 1929. The 1928 values of income and product variables which enter the model as initial lags were derived from unpublished tables, developed in connection with another study, by Harold Barger and L. R. Klein. These unpublished data are obtained essentially by splicing the USDC series and corresponding earlier estimates by S. Kuznets and Barger.

PERSONAL TAX-TRANSFER ITEMS

The U.S. Department of Commerce calculates *aggregate* disposable income, but not disposable income by distributive shares, which are the appropriate ones for demand variables in our model: e.g., $W_1+W_2-T_W$, $P-T_P$, $A_1+A_2-T_A$. The current dollar values of T_W, T_P, and T_A are obtained by allocating to the appropriate distributive share the tax and transfer items which bridge the gap between national income and disposable income in the National Accounts. This allocation is described in an article by L. Frane and L. R. Klein. [1]) The procedure

---

[1]) L. Frane and L. R. Klein, "The Estimation of Disposable Income by Distributive Shares," *Review of Economics and Statistics*, Vol. XXXV, 1953, pp. 333–37.

used there for 1929–1950 was applied to 1928, 1951, and 1952 also; and the 1949–1950 allocation was revised on the basis of later data. Table 3 of that article presents figures identical with the current dollar estimates of $W_1+W_2-T_W$, $P-S_P-T_P$, and $A_1+A_2-T_A$, except for the adjustment of profits to reflect replacement cost depreciation. [1])

Stock of Capital

Starting from 1928 $= 0$ as an arbitrary origin, our series on the stock of capital is obtained by cumulating net investment. There is some difficulty in carrying this procedure through the war years into the postwar portion of our sample period. Because of accelerated depreciation provisions of the tax law and postwar sales of surplus government assets, it would presumably understate the actual postwar stock of capital. Instead, we bridge the war years by the stock of capital figures for 1940 and 1946 estimated by Raymond Goldsmith. [2])

Liquid Asset Holdings

The Federal Reserve Board publishes, for the years since 1939, the December 31 holdings of liquid assets, (broken down into currency, demand deposits, time deposits, saving and loan shares, and U.S. Government securities), by type of holder (broken down into persons, corporations, and unincorporated businesses).

The 1928–1938 figures used were obtained by extrapolations of these components by types of holders, using indices constructed from studies of Irwin Friend, Raymond Goldsmith, and Solomon Shapiro, and guided by a detailed description of the methods used by the Federal Reserve Board in deriving its current series.

---

[1]) In addition, we now include farm corporations in the farm, rather than the business sector. In the later sections of the appendixes, we will generally not explicitly mention this minor item; for all the sample and post-sample years, farm corporate profits are included in farm income rather than in the business sector.

[2]) Goldsmith made no explicit adjustment for transfer of surplus war assets from the public to the private sector. He does, however, use a method of constructing a series on capital which avoids the problem of accelerated depreciation.

Sources of Data

In this section we list in detail the sources of data for the sample period 1929–1941, 1946–1952 used in the re-estimation of the structural parameters of the model, which was described in Chapter VI. In the original estimation from the 1929–1941, 1946–1950 sample period, essentially the same sources and procedures were followed, with the data for the most recent years of the period being preliminary.

$Y+T+D$: Gross National Product, billions of 1939 dollars.

$$Y+T+D = (1)$$

C: Consumer Expenditures, billions of 1939 dollars.

$$C = (2)$$

I: Gross Private Domestic Capital Formation, billions of 1939 dollars.

$$I = (3)$$

G: Government Expenditures for Goods and Services, billions of 1939 dollars.

$$G = (4) - \frac{(5)}{(6)}$$

p: Price Index of Gross National Product, 1939: 100.

$$p = 100 \times (6)$$

F_E: Exports of Goods and Services, billions of 1939 dollars.

$$F_E = (7)$$

F_I: Imports of Goods and Services, billions of 1939 dollars.

$$F_I = (8) - \frac{(5)}{(6)}$$

W_1:   Private Employee Compensation, Deflated, billions of dollars.

W_1 = National Income figure in unpublished tables, Harold Barger, allocated to distributive shares according to 1929 distribution, adjusted to 1928 on basis of data in Simon Kuznets, *National Income and Its Composition*, (New York: National Bureau of

Economic Research 1941) deflated by (6) $t = 1928$

$$W_1 = \frac{(9) + (10)}{(6)} \qquad t > 1928$$

W_2: Government Employee Compensation, Deflated, billions of dollars.

W_2 = National Income figure in unpublished tables, Harold Barger, allocated to distributive shares on basis of data in Simon Kuznets, *op. cit.*, deflated by (6) $t = 1928$

$$W_2 = \frac{(11) + (12)}{(6)} \qquad t > 1928.$$

P: Nonwage Nonfarm Income, Deflated, billions of dollars.

P = National Income figure in unpublished tables, Harold Barger, allocated to distributive shares on basis of data in Simon Kuznets, *op. cit.*, deflated by (6) $t = 1928$

$$P = \frac{(13)+(14)+(15)+(16)+(17)+(18)}{(6)} - D \quad t > 1928.$$

A_1: Farm Income, Deflated, billions of dollars.

A_1 = National Income figure in unpublished tables, Harold Barger, allocated to distributive shares on basis of data in Simon Kuznets, *op. cit.*, deflated by (6) $t = 1928$

$$A_1 = \frac{(19) + (20) - [(21) - (22)]}{(6)} \qquad t > 1928.$$

A_2: Government Payments to Farmers, Deflated, billions of dollars.

$$A_2 = \frac{(21) - (22)}{(6)}$$

A: Farm Income (old concept), Deflated, billions of dollars.

$$A = A_1 + A_2$$

Note: This is the farm income variable used in the first estimation of the model.

D: Capital Consumption Charges (at replacement cost), billions of 1939 dollars.

D = Current dollar figure extrapolated back from 1929 on the basis of unpublished tables, Harold Barger, deflated by (28) $t = 1928$

$$D = \frac{\dfrac{(23) - (24)}{(25)} + (24) + (26) + (27)}{(28)} \qquad t > 1928.$$

Note: (24), (26), (27) are already on replacement cost basis and need not be revalued.

P_C: Corporate Profits, Deflated, billions of dollars.

P_C = Current dollar figure extrapolated back from 1929 on the basis of unpublished tables, Harold Barger, deflated by (6) $t = 1928$

$$P_C = \frac{(15) + (16)}{(6)} + (29)\left(\frac{(18)}{(6)} - D\right) \qquad t > 1928.$$

S_P: Corporate Savings, Deflated, billions of dollars.

S_P = Current dollar figure extrapolated back from 1929 on the basis of unpublished tables, Harold Barger, deflated by (6) $t = 1928$

$$S_P = \frac{(30) + (16)}{(6)} + (29)\left(\frac{(18)}{(6)} - D\right) \qquad t > 1928$$

T: Indirect Taxes less Subsidies, Deflated, billions of dollars.

$$T = \frac{(31) + (32) + (33) - (34)}{(6)}$$

T_W: Personal and Payroll Taxes less Transfers Associated with Wage and Salary Income, Deflated, billions of dollars.

$$T_W = \frac{(35)}{(6)}$$

T_P: Personal and Corporate Taxes less Transfers Associated with Nonwage Nonfarm Income, Deflated, billions of dollars.

$$T_P = \frac{(36)}{(6)}$$

T_C: Corporate Income Taxes, Deflated, billions of dollars.

$$T_C = \frac{(37)}{(6)}$$

T_A: Taxes less Transfers Associated with Farm Income, Deflated, billions of dollars.

$$T_A = \frac{(38)}{(6)}$$

B: End-of-Year Corporate Surplus, Deflated, billions of dollars, from arbitrary origin.

$$B_t = 0 \qquad\qquad\qquad t = 1928$$

$$B_t = \sum_{i=1929}^{t} (S_P)_i \qquad\qquad t > 1928$$

K: End-of-Year Stock of Private Capital, billions of 1939 dollars, from arbitrary origin.

$$K_t = 0 \qquad\qquad\qquad t = 1928$$

$$K_t = \sum_{i=1929}^{t} (I_i - D_i) \qquad\qquad 1929 \le t \le 1941$$

$$K_t = K_{1946} - I_{1946} + D_{1946} \qquad t = 1945$$

$$K_{1946} = K_{1940} + (K^*_{1946} - K^*_{1940})$$

$$K_t = K_{1946} + \sum_{i=1947}^{t} (I_i - D_i) \quad t > 1946$$

Note: K^* is the series derived from Raymond W. Goldsmith, "A Perpetual Inventory of National Wealth," *Studies in Income and Wealth*, Volume XIV, (New York: National Bureau of Economic Research, 1951), Table 1B. The figures for these components of national wealth; Structures (except Institution and Government), Producers' Durables, and Private Inventories; were summed and converted to 1939 dollars by (28).

F_A: Index of Agricultural Exports, 1939: 100.

$$F_A = \frac{(39)}{.58}, \text{ to shift index from 1924–1929 : 100 to 1939 : 100}$$

p_A:　　Index of Agricultural Prices, 1939: 100.

$$p_A = \frac{(40)}{.95}, \text{ to shift index from } 1910\text{--}1914:100 \text{ to } 1939:100$$

p_I:　　Index of Prices of Imports, 1939: 100.

$$p_I = (41) \times \left[\frac{1.00 + (42)}{1.1441} \right]$$

Note: Multiplication of (41) by the bracketed expression converts the index to one of import prices after duties.

N_P:　　Number of Persons in the United States, millions of persons.

$$N_P = (43)$$

N:　　Number of Persons in the Labor Force, millions of persons

$N\ = (44)$ 　　　　　　　　　　　　　　$t \leq 1939$

$N\ = (44) + 0.150$, $t > 1939$, to allow for 150,000 members of armed forces who were outside the continental U.S. in 1940 and who were therefore not enumerated in the 1940 census. This figure is deducted by the Census Bureau from its current estimates.

N_W:　　Number of Wage- and Salary-Earners, millions of persons.

$$N_W = (45)$$

N_G:　　Number of Government Employees, millions of persons.

$$N_G = (46)$$

N_F:　　Number of Farm Operators, millions of persons.

$$N_F = (47)$$

N_E:　　Number of Nonfarm Entrepreneurs, millions of persons.

$$N_E = (48)$$

h:　　Index of Hours Worked per Year, 1939: 1.00.

$$h\ = \frac{(49)}{40.4} \qquad\qquad t \leq 1949$$

Division by 40.4 converts this series from units of hours per week to an index with base value 1939: 1.00.

$$h\ = \frac{p(W_1 + W_2)}{wN_W} \qquad\qquad t > 1949$$

w: Index of Hourly Wages, 1939: 122.1.

w Extrapolated back from 1929 figure by same percentage change as (51) $t = 1928$

$w = (50)$ $1928 < t \leq 1949$

$w = \{- 9.2 + 1.11[(51)]\} \times 1.221$ $t > 1949.$

Note: For years after 1949 w is computed from regression equation between (51) and $\dfrac{(50)}{1.221}$, based on 1929–1949 data; then converted from 1939: 100 to 1939: 122.1.

i_L: Average Yield on Corporate Bonds, Percent per annum.

$$i_L = (52)$$

i_S: Average Yield on Short Term Commercial Paper, Percent per annum.

$$i_S = (53)$$

R: Excess Reserves of Banks as a Percentage of Total Reserves, Percent.

$$R = \frac{(54)}{(55)}$$

L_1: End-of-Year Liquid Assets Held by Persons, Deflated, billions of dollars.

$$L_1 = \frac{(56) - (57) + (59) - (60) + .95 \times (62)}{(6)} \qquad t \leq 1938$$

$$L_1 = \frac{(63)}{(6)} \qquad t > 1938$$

L_2: End-of-Year Liquid Assets Held by Businesses, Deflated, billions of dollars.

$$L_2 = \frac{(57) + (58) + (60) + (61) + .03 \times (62)}{(6)} \qquad t \leq 1938$$

$$L_2 = \frac{(64)}{(6)} \qquad t > 1938$$

t: Time in Years, from arbitrary origin, 1929 : 0.

(1) Gross National Product, billions of 1939 dollars
1928: Unpublished tables, Harold Barger
1929–1952: U.S. Department of Commerce, National Accounts, Table A

(2) Personal Consumption Expenditures, billions of 1939 dollars
1928: Unpublished tables, Harold Barger
1929–1952: U.S. Department of Commerce, National Accounts, Table A

(3) Gross Private Domestic Investment, billions of 1939 dollars
1929–1952: U.S. Department of Commerce, National Accounts, Table A

(4) Government Purchases of Goods and Services, billions of 1939 dollars
1929–1952: U.S. Department of Commerce, National Accounts, Table A

(5) Sales of the Rest of the World to U.S. Government, billions of current dollars
1928: Unilateral transfers abroad, U.S. Department of Commerce, *The Balance of International Payments of the U.S. 1946–1948*, p. 272
1929–1952: U.S. Department of Commerce, National Accounts, Table 11
Note: In the original estimation of the model, this item was represented by Net Government Unilateral Transfers:
1928–1941: U.S. Department of Commerce, *The Balance of International Payments of the United States 1946–1948*, p. 275
1945–1950: *Statistical Abstract of the United States 1951*, p. 817

(6) Implicit Price Deflator of Gross National Product, 1939: 1.00
1927–1928: Unpublished tables, Harold Barger
1929–1952: U.S. Department of Commerce, National Accounts, Table B

(7) Export Component of Net Foreign Investment, billions of 1939 dollars
1929–1952: U.S. Department of Commerce, private correspondence
Note: Net Foreign Investment (exports less imports) in billions of 1939 dollars is published by the U.S. Department of Commerce, National Accounts, Table A. The breakdown between exports and imports was obtained in private correspondence. Exports in current dollars can be obtained directly as the sum of the following items in Table 11 of the National Accounts: Net payments of factor income, purchases from United States Government, purchases from United States persons, and purchases from United States business.

(8) Import Component of Net Foreign Investment, billions of 1939 dollars
1928: U.S. Department of Commerce, *The Balance of International Payments of the U.S. 1946–1948*, p. 272. Imports of Goods, Other Services, and Unilateral Transfers Abroad, deflated by Index of Import Prices computed from regression equation, fitted to 1929–1950 observations, of Implicit Price Deflator of Import Component of Net Foreign Investment on the Index of Unit Value of Imports published in *Survey of Current Business*, July, 1951, pp. 27–28.

1929–1952: U.S. Department of Commerce, private correspondence

Note: Imports in current dollars can be obtained directly as the sum of the following items in Table 11 of the National Accounts: Sales to United States business, sales to United States Government, and sales to United States persons.

(9) Wages and Salaries: All industries except Government and Government Enterprises, billions of current dollars
1929–1952: U.S. Department of Commerce, National Accounts, Table 14

(10) Supplements to Wages and Salaries: All industries except Government and Government Enterprises, billions of current dollars
1929–1952: U.S. Department of Commerce, National Accounts, Table 15

(11) Wages and Salaries: Government and Government Enterprises, billions of current dollars
1929–1952: U.S. Department of Commerce, National Accounts, Table 14

(12) Supplements to Wages and Salaries: Government and Government Enterprises, billions of current dollars
1929–1952: U.S. Department of Commerce, National Accounts, Table 15

(13) Income of Unincorporated Enterprises and Inventory Valuation Adjustment: Business and Professional, billions of current dollars
1929–1952: U.S. Department of Commerce, National Accounts, Table 1

(14) Rental Income of Persons, billions of current dollars
1929–1952: U.S. Department of Commerce, National Accounts, Table 1

(15) Corporate Profits before Federal and State Income and Excess Profits Taxes: All industries except farms, billions of current dollars
1929–1952: U.S. Department of Commerce, National Accounts, Table 17

(16) Inventory Valuation Adjustment: Corporations, billions of current dollars
1929–1952: U.S. Department of Commerce, National Accounts, Table 22A

(17) Net Interest, billions of current dollars
1929–1952: U.S. Department of Commerce, National Accounts, Table 1

(18) Capital Consumption Allowances (at original cost), billions of current dollars
1929–1952: U.S. Department of Commerce, National Accounts, Table 4
Note: (18) = (23) + (26) + (27)

(19) Income of Unincorporated Enterprises: Farm, billions of current dollars
1929–1952: U.S. Department of Commerce, National Accounts, Table 1
Note: Net proceeds to farmers from Commodity Credit Corporation non-recourse loans are included.

(20) Corporate Profits Before Federal and State Income and Excess Profits Taxes: Farms, billions of current dollars
1929–1952: U.S. Department of Commerce, National Accounts, Table 17

125

(21) Government Payments to Farmers, billions of current dollars
1928–1952: U.S. Bureau of Agricultural Economics, *Agricultural Statistics 1953*, p. 609.

Note: Includes payments under rental and benefit, soil conservation, price adjustment, price parity, Sugar Act, and production programs. The net proceeds to farmers from Commodity Credit Corporation non-recourse loans, data for which are not available separately, are *not* included.

(22) Government Payments received by landlords not living on farms, billions of current dollars
1928–1952: U.S. Bureau of Agricultural Economics, *Agricultural Statistics 1953*, p. 617.

(23) Depreciation Charges, billions of current dollars
1929–1952: U.S. Department of Commerce, National Accounts, Table 4

(24) Agricultural Depreciation Charges, billions of current dollars
1929–1951: U.S. Department of Commerce, private correspondence
1952: U.S. Bureau of Agricultural Economics, private correspondence; percentage change in this series 1951–1952 used to extrapolate Department of Commerce series beyond 1951

(25) Ratio of Depreciation Charges at Original Cost to Depreciation Charges at Replacement Cost, pure number
1929–1949: Raymond Goldsmith, *A Study of Saving in the United States*, (Princeton, 1954).
1950–1952: Computed from regression equation fitted to 1929–1949 data:

$$y = -\,6.718 + 2.24x; \text{ where } y = \frac{(23)-(24)}{(25)},\ x = (23)-(24)$$

(26) Accidental Damage to Fixed Capital, billions of current dollars
1929–1952: U.S. Department of Commerce, National Accounts, Table 4

(27) Capital Outlays Charged to Current Expense, billions of current dollars
1929–1952: U.S. Department of Commerce, National Accounts, Table 4

(28) Implicit Price Deflator of Gross Private Domestic Investment, 1939: 1.00
1928: Unpublished Tables, Harold Barger
1929–1952: U.S. Department of Commerce, National Accounts, Table B

(29) Ratio of Corporate to Total Nonfarm Depreciation Charges, pure number
1929–1951: U.S. Department of Commerce, private correspondence
1952: Assumed at 1951 value
Note: The breakdown which was obtained for all years in private correspondence has been published for 1947 only as Exhibit 35 in U.S. Department of Commerce, *Survey of Current Business: 1951 National Income Supplement*, p. 138.

(30) Undistributed Corporate Income: All industries except farms, billions of current dollars
1929–1952: U.S. Department of Commerce, National Accounts, Table 21

(31) Indirect Business Tax and Non-Tax Liability, billions of current dollars
1929–1952: U.S. Department of Commerce, National Accounts, Table 4

(32) Business Transfer Payments, billions of current dollars
1928: Unpublished tables, Harold Barger
1929–1952: U.S. Department of Commerce, National Accounts, Table 4

(33) Statistical Discrepancy between the Product and Income Sides of the National Accounts, billions of current dollars
1928: Unpublished tables, Harold Barger
1929–1952: U.S. Department of Commerce, National Accounts, Table 4

(34) Subsidies Minus Current Surplus of Government Enterprises, billions of current dollars
1928: Unpublished tables, Harold Barger
1929–1952: U.S. Department of Commerce, National Accounts, Table 4

(35) Taxes Less Transfer Payments: Wage and Salary Income, billions of current dollars
1928–1952: See page 116 above

(36) Taxes less Transfer Payments: Nonwage Nonfarm Income, billions of current dollars
1928–1952: See page 116 above

(37) Federal and State Corporate Income and Excess Profits Tax Liability: All industries except farms, billions of current dollars
1928: Unpublished Tables, Harold Barger
1929–1952: U.S. Department of Commerce, National Accounts, Table 18

(38) Taxes Less Transfer Payments: Farm Income, billions of current dollars
1928–1952: See page 116 above

(39) Index of Quantity of Exports of Total Agricultural Products; monthly average 1924–1929: 100
1929–1934: U.S. Department of Commerce, *Survey of Current Business*: *1942 Statistical Supplement*, p. 88
1935–1952: U.S. Department of Commerce, *Business Statistics 1953*, p. 104

(40) Index of Prices Received by Farmers, 1910–1914: 100
1928–1951: U.S. Bureau of Agricultural Economics, *Agricultural Statistics 1952*, pp. 618–619
1952: U.S. Department of Commerce, *Business Statistics 1953*, p. 25

127

(41) Implicit Price Deflator of Import Component of Net Foreign Investment, 1939: 100
    1929–1952: U.S. Department of Commerce, private correspondence

(42) Ratio of Duties Calculated to Total Value of Free and Dutiable Imports, pure number
    1929–1939: U.S. Department of Commerce, *Historical Statistics of the United States: 1789–1945*, p. 247, Series M-72
    1940–1941: U.S. Department of Commerce, *Statistical Abstract of the United States 1951*, p. 854
    1946–1951: U.S. Department of the Treasury, *Annual Report of the Secretary of the Treasury 1952*, p. 715
    1952: Extrapolated on the basis of figures for the first six months in *Annual Report of the Secretary of the Treasury 1952*, p. 715

(43) Population of Continental United States, including armed forces overseas, July 1, millions of persons
    1929–1952: U.S. Department of Commerce, *Statistical Abstract of the United States 1953*, p. 13

(44) Labor Force, including armed forces, millions of persons
    1929–1952: U.S. Department of Commerce, *Statistical Abstract of the United States 1953*, p. 186.

(45) Average Number of Full-Time and Part-Time Employees, millions of persons
    1929–1952: U.S. Department of Commerce, National Accounts, Table 25

(46) Average Number of Full-Time and Part-Time Employees: Government and government enterprises, millions of persons
    1929–1952: U.S. Department of Commerce, National Accounts, Table 25

(47) Number of Active Proprietors of Unincorporated Enterprises: Farms, millions of persons
    1929–1952: U.S. Department of Commerce, National Accounts, Table 27

(48) Number of Active Proprietors of Unincorporated Enterprises: All industries except farms, millions of persons
    1929–1952: U.S. Department of Commerce, National Accounts, Table 27

(49) Combined Weekly Hours, hours per week
    1929–1949: Colin Clark, *Review of Economic Progress*, Vol. 3, No. 3, March 1951, p. 5

(50) Index of Hourly Wages, 1939: 122.1
$$1929\text{–}1949: \frac{p(W_1 + W_2)}{hN_W}$$

(51) Index of Average Hourly Earnings of Wage Earners, 1939: 100
    1928–1937: "Index of Wages," converted from 1926: 100 to 1939: 100 Federal Reserve Bank of New York, Mimeographed Release, January 1942

1938–1952: Federal Reserve Bank of New York, Mimeographed Releases

Note: These indexes, currently issued in monthly releases, are discussed in: George Garvy and Robert E. Lewis, "New Indexes of Hourly and Weekly Earnings Compiled by the Federal Reserve Bank of New York," *Journal of the American Statistical Association*, Vol. 42, June, 1947, pp. 256–70.

(52) Moody's Total Corporate Bond Yield, percent per annum

1928–1941: *Banking and Monetary Statistics*, Board of Governors of Federal Reserve System, p. 468.

1946–1952: *Federal Reserve Bulletins*, Board of Governors of Federal Reserve System

(53) Interest Rate on Prime Commercial Paper, 4- to 6-months, percent per annum

1924–1941: *Banking and Monetary Statistics*, Board of Governors of Federal Reserve System, p. 448

1942–1952: *Federal Reserve Bulletins*, Board of Governors of Federal Reserve System

(54) Excess Reserve Balances of Member Banks, annual average of daily figures, billions of current dollars

1929–1941: *Banking and Monetary Statistics*, Board of Governors of Federal Reserve System, p. 368.

1946–1952: Board of Governors of Federal Reserve System, private correspondence. Monthly averages of daily figures are published in the *Federal Reserve Bulletins*, Board of Governors of Federal Reserve System

(55) Total Reserve Balances of Member Banks, annual average of daily figures, billions of current dollars

1929–1941: *Banking and Monetary Statistics*, Board of Governors of Federal Reserve System, p. 368.

1946–1948: Average of monthly averages of daily figures in E. A. Goldenweiser, *American Monetary Policy*, (New York: Mc Graw-Hill, 1951) pp. 321–324

1949–1952: Board of Governors of Federal Reserve System, Private correspondence

(56) Noncorporate Holdings of Currency, Demand Deposits, a.:d Time Deposits, billions of current dollars

1928–1938: 1939 Federal Reserve figure, component of (63), extrapolated back by index of the series covering personal and unincorporated business holdings given in Irwin Friend, *Individuals' Saving*, (New York: John Wiley and Sons, 1954).

(57) Unincorporated Business Holdings of Currency, Demand Deposits, and Time Deposits, billions of current dollars

1928–1938: 1939 Federal Reserve figure, component of (63), extrapolated back by index of the series given in Solomon Shapiro: "The Distribution of Deposits and Currency in the United States, 1929–1939," *Journal of the American Statistical Association*, Vol. XXXVIII, Dec., 1943, pp. 438 ff. For 1928, Raymond Goldsmith's series on Cash of Non-Corporate Business given in *A Study of Saving in the United States* were used to extrapolate back Shapiro's 1929 figure.

(58) Corporate Business Holdings of Currency, Demand Deposits, and Time Deposits, billions of current dollars

1928–1938: 1939 Federal Reserve figure, component of (63), extrapolated back by index of the series given in Friend, *op. cit.*. For 1928–1931 the series given in Friedrich Lutz, *Corporate Cash Balances 1914–1943*, (New York: National Bureau of Economic Research, 1945), p. 113 was used to extrapolate back Friend's 1932 figure.

(59) Noncorporate Holdings of U.S. Government Securities, billions of current dollars

1928–1938: 1939 Federal Reserve figure, component of (63) extrapolated back by index of the series given in Friend, *op. cit.*.

(60) Unincorporated Business Holdings of U.S. Government Securities, billions of current dollars

1928–1938: 1939 Federal Reserve figure, component of (63), extrapolated back by index of the series given in Goldsmith, *op. cit.*.

(61) Corporate Business Holdings of U.S. Government Securities, billions of current dollars

1928–1938: 1939 Federal Reserve figure, component of (63), extrapolated back by index of the series given in Friend, *op. cit.*. For 1928–1931, the "Other Investors" holdings given in *Banking and Monetary Statistics*, Table 149, p. 512, interpolated to December 31, adjusted for holdings of insurance companies, state and local governments, and noncorporate units, was used to extrapolate back Friend's 1932 figure.

(62) Private Share Capital of All Operating Savings and Loan Associations, billions of current dollars

1928–1938: Federal Home Loan Board, *Federal Home Loan Bank Review 1947 Statistical Supplement*, p. 7, allocated 2% excluded holders, 95% personal holdings, 3% business holdings in accordance with 1939 distribution given by Board of Governors of Federal Reserve System, "Derivation of Liquid Asset Distribution Estimates" mimeographed release R&S 1147.

(63) Liquid Asset Holdings: Personal, billions of current dollars

1939–1952: Board of Governors of Federal Reserve System, *Federal Reserve Bulletin*, July, 1953, p. 720.

(64) Liquid Asset Holdings: Business, billions of current dollars
1939–1952: Board of Governors of Federal Reserve System, *Federal Reserve Bulletin*, July, 1953, p. 720.

Sample Data

	$Y+T+D$	C	I	G	$p^1)$	F_E	F_I	W_1	W_2	P	A_1	A_2
1928	79.8	58.4			122.6		3.9	35.02	3.89	19.80	4.47	0.00
1929	85.9	62.2	14.9	7.8	120.9	5.0	4.1	37.78	4.23	23.00	4.69	0.00
1930	78.1	58.6	10.1	8.6	116.3	4.3	3.6	35.41	4.59	18.86	3.35	0.00
1931	72.3	56.6	5.9	9.3	105.0	3.6	3.2	32.40	5.19	13.80	2.70	0.00
1932	61.9	51.8	1.1	8.8	94.2	2.9	2.7	27.23	5.49	8.96	1.75	0.00
1933	61.5	51.1	1.6	8.6	90.7	2.9	2.8	26.44	5.90	7.90	2.36	0.12
1934	67.9	54.0	3.5	10.0	95.5	3.1	2.7	29.08	6.59	10.76	1.99	0.42
1935	73.9	57.2	6.7	10.0	97.7	3.3	3.3	31.07	6.91	14.19	4.49	0.51
1936	83.9	62.8	9.3	11.8	98.3	3.4	3.5	35.14	8.27	17.10	3.71	0.25
1937	87.9	65.0	11.4	11.3	102.7	4.1	4.0	38.85	7.59	18.65	5.20	0.28
1938	84.0	63.9	6.3	12.6	100.9	4.2	3.1	35.88	8.47	17.09	4.00	0.37
1939	91.3	67.5	9.9	13.0	100.0	4.2	3.3	39.27	8.55	19.28	3.85	0.66
1940	100.0	71.3	13.7	13.7	101.5	4.9	3.6	42.35	8.67	23.24	4.26	0.62
1941	115.5	76.6	17.1	20.8	109.5	5.0	4.0	49.13	9.58	28.11	5.94	0.43
1945	153.4	86.3	8.3		140.3		4.6	61.01	26.68	30.29	8.49	0.47
1946	138.4	95.7	20.3	18.9	152.6	7.5	4.0	61.88	14.85	28.26	9.31	0.45
1947	138.6	98.3	19.3	15.6	168.3	9.4	4.0	64.91	11.00	27.91	9.15	0.16
1948	143.5	100.3	22.7	17.9	180.6	7.2	4.6	66.75	10.87	32.30	9.72	0.13
1949	144.0	103.2	18.0	20.0	179.4	7.4	4.6	65.84	12.17	31.39	7.12	0.09
1950	156.2	108.9	26.8	19.0	183.6	7.1	5.4	70.85	12.72	35.61	7.25	0.14
1951	167.0	108.5	27.6	27.5	197.5	8.6	5.2	75.38	15.21	37.58	7.85	0.13
1952	172.0	111.4	24.3	33.4	202.4	8.3	5.5	78.65	16.82	35.17	7.30	0.12

[1]) Values for these years appeared as lags for the sample period:

| 1927 | 122.9 | 1944 | 136.2 |

	A	D	P_C	S_P	T	T_W	T_P	T_C	T_A	B	K
1928	4.47	9.50	6.16	0.84		−0.30	1.23	1.10	0.08	0.00	0.0
1929	4.69	9.84	6.98	1.02	6.33	−0.30	1.69	1.15	0.09	1.02	5.1
1930	3.35	9.81	4.30	−1.15	6.11	−0.37	1.18	0.73	0.10	− 0.13	5.4
1931	2.70	9.89	0.42	−3.95	8.33	−1.56	0.31	0.48	0.09	− 4.08	1.4
1932	1.75	8.96	−2.54	−5.67	9.54	−1.28	−0.13	0.40	0.08	− 9.75	− 6.5
1933	2.49	8.90	−2.69	−5.55	9.85	−1.25	0.06	0.58	0.05	−15.30	−13.8
1934	2.41	9.62	−0.01	−3.49	9.46	−1.21	0.32	0.78	0.02	−18.79	−19.9
1935	5.00	8.50	2.51	−1.40	8.22	−1.29	0.92	0.98	0.00	−20.19	−21.7
1936	3.95	9.18	4.24	−1.79	10.25	−2.10	1.69	1.42	0.02	−21.97	−21.6
1937	5.48	8.87	5.37	−0.64	8.39	0.38	2.14	1.46	0.00	−22.61	−19.1
1938	4.37	8.89	3.73	−0.45	9.23	0.19	1.62	1.03	0.00	−23.07	−21.7
1939	4.51	9.02	5.23	−0.01	10.71	0.16	1.70	1.46	0.00	−23.07	−20.8
1940	4.88	9.30	8.47	1.67	11.48	0.23	3.08	2.83	−0.02	−21.40	−16.4
1941	6.37	10.10	12.37	1.17	12.14	0.93	7.76	7.14	0.00	−20.23	− 9.4
1945	8.96	12.07	11.50	0.21		8.72	10.96	7.95	0.54	−15.56	−11.4
1946	9.76	11.32	10.09	0.06	12.23	3.19	8.44	6.23	0.49	−15.49	− 2.4
1947	9.32	13.46	12.08	1.19	11.72	3.99	9.17	7.04	0.45	−14.31	3.4
1948	9.85	13.69	15.33	4.18	9.99	3.61	8.95	7.17	0.55	−10.13	12.4
1949	7.31	14.75	14.09	3.92	12.60	2.50	7.27	6.03	0.36	− 6.21	15.6
1950	7.52	16.25	17.09	2.27	13.39	2.60	11.22	9.88	0.37	− 3.94	26.1
1951		17.06	18.72	2.23	13.79	7.15	14.64	11.88	0.33	− 1.71	36.6
1952		19.35	16.51	1.90	14.51	8.63	13.72	10.14	0.38	0.19	41.5

	F_A	p_A	p_I	N_P	N	N_W	N_G	N_F	N_E	t
1928		157								
1929	162	156	143.6	121.8	49.4	37.0	3.6	5.6	4.8	0
1930	138	132	123.6	123.1	50.1	35.0	3.7	5.7	4.8	1
1931	134	92	101.4	124.0	50.7	32.1	4.1	5.8	4.8	2
1932	118	68	82.9	124.8	51.3	28.8	4.3	5.9	4.7	3
1933	131	74	79.2	125.6	51.8	30.3	5.8	6.0	4.6	4
1934	102	95	90.7	126.4	52.5	33.5	6.8	6.1	4.6	5
1935	95	115	96.2	127.3	53.1	34.9	7.1	5.9	4.7	6
1936	88	120	96.6	128.1	53.7	37.9	8.0	5.7	4.8	7
1937	102	128	104.7	128.8	54.3	39.1	7.1	5.5	4.9	8
1938	116	102	97.1	129.8	55.0	37.8	8.1	5.3	4.9	9
1939	100	100	100.0	130.9	55.6	39.2	7.9	5.2	5.0	10
1940	72	105	99.2	132.0	56.2	40.9	7.7	5.1	5.0	11
1941	66	129	107.4	133.4	57.5	45.4	8.5	5.0	4.9	12
1945		217								
1946	174	246	158.8	141.4	61.0	49.2	9.2	4.8	5.5	17
1947	183	289	183.0	144.1	61.8	49.3	7.2	5.0	5.9	18
1948	157	300	189.8	146.6	62.9	50.2	7.2	4.7	6.1	19
1949	186	262	180.2	149.0	63.7	48.9	7.6	4.7	6.1	20
1950	155	269	196.5	151.7	64.7	50.7	7.8	4.4	6.2	21
1951	184	318	244.5	154.4	66.0	54.7	9.6	4.1	6.3	22
1952	164	303	232.1	157.0	66.6	56.0	10.4	4.0	6.3	23

	h	w	i_L	i_S [1])	R	L_1	L_2
1928		117.1		4.85		36.5	15.0
1929	1.158	118.4	5.21	5.85	1.8	33.6	16.0
1930	1.109	119.9	5.09	3.59	2.3	33.9	16.0
1931	1.079	114.1	5.81	2.64	3.8	37.6	14.9
1932	1.010	105.9	6.87	2.73	12.1	40.4	16.7
1933	1.032	93.8	5.89	1.73	22.5	39.7	16.2
1934	0.990	102.7	4.96	1.02	42.5	40.5	16.8
1935	1.030	103.3	4.46	0.76	49.4	42.1	17.1
1936	1.067	105.5	3.87	0.75	41.9	45.4	18.1
1937	1.040	117.2	3.94	0.94	17.9	45.2	17.1
1938	0.941	125.6	4.19	0.81	31.8	46.2	17.7
1939	1.000	122.1	3.77	0.59	42.4	49.6	19.4
1940	1.015	124.7	3.55	0.56	47.7	51.6	22.0
1941	1.054	134.5	3.34	0.54	39.7	54.3	23.7
1945		195.1		0.75		110.1	52.0
1946	1.097	217.2	2.74	0.81	6.1	108.3	43.4
1947	1.077	241.2	2.86	1.03	5.2	102.4	38.3
1948	1.059	263.7	3.08	1.44	4.7	96.5	35.7
1949	1.033	276.9	2.96	1.48	4.6	98.3	37.2
1950	1.056	286.9	2.86	1.45	4.8	97.9	38.4
1951	1.056	309.9	3.08	2.17	3.9	93.3	37.9
1952	1.057	326.2	3.19	2.33	3.5	95.2	38.1

[1]) Values for these years appeared as lags for the sample period:

1924	3.98	1942	0.66
1925	4.02	1943	0.69
1926	4.34	1944	0.73
1927	4.11		

Sources of Data for Extrapolation and Forecasting

In a realistic forecasting situation, we are faced with two distinct data problems: 1) specifying the values of exogenous variables for the forecast period and 2) specifying the values of lagged endogenous variables for the forecast period. When the forecast is made before the beginning of the forecast period T, estimates of the values for the period $T - 1$ of variables which appear as lags in the model must be made. Even when the forecast period has already begun, values of lagged variables will have to be estimated because of the time lags

133

between the collection, preparation, and final publication of the official series. This lag is often so long that this second problem is present even in the making of "ex-post forecasts," i.e. extrapolation to post sample periods, such as those described in Chapter V. As a rule, however, related series are available on which to base the estimates of the variables of our model.

In this section we will only briefly indicate the general nature of the material used in making these estimates. The actual values of our estimates have been given at the appropriate points in the preceding chapters.

EXTRAPOLATIONS TO 1951 AND 1952

We tested our first estimated model by making ex-post forecasts to two post-sample years during December 1952 and January and February 1953. By that time, a comprehensive set of national accounts for 1951 had been published. [1]) Similarly we had virtually complete official coverage of 1951 values of the other variables – population, employment, liquid assets, interest rates, etc. – of the system. Hence, essentially the same sources and procedures were employed to obtain 1951 values as were used for the sample period. Values for 1950 which appeared as lags in the 1951 extrapolation had already been prepared as sample period observations.

While the official Department of Commerce national accounts for 1952 had not yet appeared, the President's Council of Economic Advisers had published preliminary estimates. [2]) Some of our items appeared only implicitly (e.g. the general price level had to be obtained as the ratio of GNP in current dollars to that in 1939 dollars). Again we followed the standard procedures. In several cases the detailed breakdowns had not been prepared. For these we used other materials to extrapolate the 1951 values of these variables, or allocated known 1952 totals to their components according to their known 1951 distributions. Items obtained by such means included the components of capital consumption allowances, the breakdowns of personal taxes and nontaxes, and the division of the total wage bill between private

---

[1]) U.S. Department of Commerce, *Survey of Current Business*, July 1952, pp. 8–31.
[2]) *The Economic Report of the President*, January 1953, Appendices A and B.

industry and government. Employment variables were extrapolated from their 1951 levels according to the movements in the corresponding series of the U.S. Census Bureau's *Monthly Review of the Labor Force*. Total liquid asset holdings were extrapolated by series appearing in the *Federal Reserve Bulletin* on adjusted demand and time deposits of all banks, currency outside banks, public ownership of U.S. government securities, and savings and loan share capital. The total for each item was allocated between personal and business holdings in the same proportion as had been observed in 1951. Values for 1951 which appeared as lags in making 1952 forecasts had been prepared as indicated in the preceding paragraph.

FORECASTS FOR 1953

Our forecasts for 1953 were made during February and March of that year. The 1952 values of variables which entered as lags had been obtained as noted in the preceding section. In this case we were in a realistic forecasting situation; hence, we had to predict 1953 values for the exogenous variables. This was done as follows: The population and employment variables N_P, N, N_E, N_F and N_G were obtained from projections made by the Council of Economic Advisers. [1]) Where our concepts differed, the Council's projections were used as extrapolators of 1952 values of our variables. The index of hours worked was held constant at its 1952 value. The import price and agricultural export indices were reduced from their 1952 levels on the basis of projections by the U.S. Departments of Commerce and Agriculture. The current dollar value of exports was held constant at its 1952 level. We used estimates of government purchases of goods and services in current dollars based on an analysis made by our colleague, R. A. Musgrave, of the budget commitments. The proportion of these purchases consisting of government payrolls was assumed to be the same as in 1952. We considered an alternative fiscal policy involving a 5% reduction in the federal budget; reducing government purchases, government payrolls, and government employment proportionately. While the government purchases (G), government payrolls (W_2), and exports (F_E) variables of our model are in constant dollars, all these money measures

---

[1]) *The Economic Report of the President*, January 1953, pp. 82–83.

were estimated in current dollars, representable as F_E^*, G^*, and W_2^*. Therefore, we also estimated separate price indexes,

$$p_G = ap \quad \text{and} \quad p_E = bp$$

respectively, where a was the average of the 1951 and 1952 observations of $\dfrac{p_G}{p}$, and b the average of the 1951 and 1952 observations of $\dfrac{p_E}{p}$.

Then we entered the variables as $\dfrac{F_E^*}{ap}$, $\dfrac{G^*}{bp}$, $\dfrac{W_2^*}{p}$ respectively, in making our forecasts for 1953.

FORECASTS FOR 1954

Our forecasts for 1954 were made with the re-estimated version of the model in November and December of 1953. In obtaining 1953 values of variables entering as lags, we estimated the annual figures on the basis of data for the portion of the year already completed. To illustrate this procedure, a necessary one in ex-ante forecasting, we present the methods used in more detail.

The USDC preliminary estimates of the components of the product side of the national accounts in current dollars for the first three quarters had appeared in the press. For GNP, personal consumption expenditures, and gross private domestic investment, we took fourth quarter values at the third quarter level. The import component of net foreign investment was extrapolated from its 1952 level by figures for the first and second quarters of the import item in the Balance of Payments. [1] Government purchases for the fourth quarter were cut 0.3 billion dollars below their third quarter level on the basis of budget commitments as analyzed by R. A. Musgrave. [2] Government purchases from abroad were continued at their 1952 level, and subtracted from the total of government expenditures on goods and services to give the current dollar value of our variable G. With the total GNP and all but one of its components estimated, that component, exports, was

---

[1] U.S. Department of Commerce, *Survey of Current Business*, September 1953, pp. 11–12.

[2] See in this respect, R. A. Musgrave, "The Fiscal Outlook," *Michigan Business Review*, Vol. VI, January 1954, pp. 18–25.

obtained as a residual. We then had consistent estimates of the current dollar values of the product side of GNP, by components.

Constant dollar estimates for the national accounts in the first three quarters had not been published. We estimated separate price indices for the components of gross national product by extrapolating our sample series from their 1952 levels with related series, which were extended at their most recently reported level through the remaining portions of 1953: For personal consumption expenditures, we extrapolated by an implicit price index of disposable personal income estimated by the Council of Economic Advisers. [1]) For the price deflator of government purchases, we extrapolated by the U.S. Department of Labor's wholesale price index. The price deflator of new construction was extrapolated by the USDC composite construction cost index; the price deflator for producers' durable equipment was extrapolated by the index of wholesale prices of machinery and motive products; the price deflator for the net change in business inventories was taken as the wholesale price index. We used the 1952 distribution of total constant dollar gross private domestic investment among its three components (construction, equipment, and inventory change) as weights, to obtain a weighted average of the separate deflators for gross private domestic investment. Import and export price deflators were extrapolated by the U.S. Department of Commerce indices of unit value of foreign trade.

Deflating each current dollar component of GNP by its respective price index, we obtained our constant dollar estimates of the components of GNP and summed these to get the constant dollar estimate of total GNP. The implicit price deflator was calculated as the ratio of current to constant dollar GNP. We used this value as the estimate of the general price level, p, in 1953.

Estimates of the income side of the national accounts had been published for only the first two quarters of 1953. We extended these through the end of the year to obtain current dollar estimates as follows: The total wage bill, $p10^{-2}(W_1 + W_2)$, was obtained as the sum of the wage and salary disbursements item of the more up-to-date monthly series on personal income (extended through the last quarter at its

---

[1]) Council of Economic Advisers, *Economic Indicators*, Oct. 1953, p. 25.

September level) and the annual rate of supplements to wages and salaries realized in the first two quarters. The government wage bill was extrapolated from its 1952 level by the government wage and salary disbursements item of personal income.

Proprietors' and rental income were also obtained from the personal income series; farm entrepreneurial income being deducted. We carried the stable item of government interest payments through the rest of the year at its second quarter level, and extrapolated dividends on the basis of 10-month estimates of the USDC. By deducting government interest and dividends from the personal interest and dividends item of the personal income series, we obtained the net interest component of the income side of the national accounts. We added nonfarm proprietors' and rental income and net interest for an estimate of noncorporate (i.e. exclusive of corporate profits and dividends) nonwage nonfarm income before inventory valuation adjustment.

USDC publication of corporate profits generally lags a full quarter behind the other components of national income. We used estimates of the National City Bank of New York [1]) to extrapolate corporate profits after tax from their 1952 level. Corporate profits taxes were extended through the year at their level for the first two quarters. Adding the profits after tax to the tax, we found profits before tax. Essentially the same figure was obtained by using a corporate profits tax function, like those developed in Appendix II, to go from profits after tax to profits before tax. Finally we added noncorporate nonwage nonfarm income to corporate profits before tax and obtained an estimate of total nonwage nonfarm income.

The annual inventory valuation adjustments for corporate and entrepreneurial income were taken at the annual rate of the first two quarters. Capital consumption allowances on an original cost basis were extended through the year with the same quarterly absolute change as had been observed between the first and second quarters. The total replacement cost depreciation adjustment and its allocation between the corporate and noncorporate sectors were obtained by the method described above for the years 1950–52. On applying these adjustments to nonwage nonfarm income and corporate profits before

[1]) *Monthly Letter on Economic Conditions, Government Finance*, November 1953, p. 123.

138

tax, we estimated the current dollar value of our variable P and P_C. We then subtracted dividends and corporate taxes from corporate profits to get corporate savings.

Government payments to farmers, $p10^{-2}A_2$, was carried at its 1952 level and deducted from farm income (obtained from the personal income series) to yield the current dollar value of our farm income variable A_1. Having thus estimated all but one component of the income side of the current dollar national accounts, and knowing the total GNP, we estimated that component, $p10^{-2}T$, as a residual.

We then used the appropriate deflators to obtain a consistent set of constant dollar national accounts for 1953. The addition of corporate savings to the corporate surplus at the end of 1952 gave corporate surplus at the end of 1953. Similarly the addition of net investment, $I - D$, to the end-of-1952 stock of capital gave the end-of-1953 stock of capital.

The personal income series (an item of which is transfer payments), available for the first three quarters, and the national accounts (available for the first two quarters), provided the basis for estimating the aggregate tax-transfer items. We extrapolated total transfer payments from their 1952 level by the corresponding item in the personal income series. Business transfer payments were estimated at their second quarter annual rate. We had already estimated contributions for social insurance and government interest payments in obtaining wage and nonwage nonfarm incomes. Federal and state and local personal taxes and nontaxes, each taken through the year at the annual rate of the second quarter, were allocated among the income shares in the same proportions as in 1952. The current dollar values of our tax-transfer variables were obtained from these estimates and then deflated by the general price level to give our variables T_W, T_P and T_A.

Our population variable, N_P, is defined as of July 1, and hence had already been published. Items reported in the USDC *Monthly Review of the Labor Force*, available through October, were used to extrapolate the labor force and employment variables N, N_W, N_G, N_E, and N_F, and the index of hours worked, h, from their 1952 levels. The money wage rate index, w, was then set to satisfy the identity:

$$\frac{w}{p} hN_W = W_1 + W_2.$$

Essentially the same estimate could have been obtained by extrapolating the index of wages and salaries of the Federal Reserve Bank of New York which was the source of the money wage rate index for the sample period.

Total liquid asset holdings were extrapolated from their 1952 level by the adjusted demand and time deposits of all banks, currency outside banks, public ownership of U.S. government securities, and savings and loan share capital series reported in the *Federal Reserve Bulletin*. The total for each item was allocated between personal and business holdings in the same proportion as had been observed in 1952; the items were added up and then deflated by the general price level to obtain the 1953 values of our variables L_1 and L_2.

Our indices of agricultural exports and farm prices were extrapolated from their 1952 levels by the reported monthly series for 1953.

These methods enabled us to assign values to the lagged endogenous variables entering our 1954 forecasting system. They also provided a basis for assigning 1954 values to many of the exogenous variables.

Population and labor force were extrapolated from 1953 to 1954 by the same absolute increase as had been observed from 1952 to 1953. The number of farmers and the number of nonfarm entrepreneurs were extrapolated from 1953 to 1954 by the same percentage change as had been observed from 1952 to 1953. The import price index was continued at its 1953 level; the farm price index at its September 1953 level; the agricultural exports index at its 1953 level (in accord with a U.S. Department of Agriculture projection). [1] The current dollar level of exports was extrapolated from 1953 to 1954 by the same absolute increase as had been observed from 1952 to 1953. (The 1953 observation used here was our best independent estimate, based on the export component of the balance of payments, rather than the export item estimated as a residual in the 1953 national accounts.) Price deflators, p_E and p_G, for exports and government purchases respectively, were taken as $p_E = ap$ and $p_G = bp$ where a and b were the averages of the 1951 to 1953 observations. The index of hours worked was cut slightly from its 1953 level when a preliminary

---

[1] U.S. Department of Agriculture, *The Demand and Price Situation*, October 1953, p. 1.

forecast, with hours constant, pointed to a slight contraction in employment.

Alternative estimates of the government items in 1954 – purchases, payrolls, and employment were made to correspond to the alternative fiscal policies we considered in making our forecasts of 1954 activity. Our central estimate was based on an implementation of the federal administration's budget through the 1954 fiscal year, i.e. through June, 1954. It had been officially indicated that "the Federal Government will purchase around $ 57 billion of goods and services in the present [1954] fiscal year, about the same amount as was purchased during fiscal year 1953." [1]) Since we already had estimates for the first half of fiscal 1954, i.e. the last two quarters of calendar 1953, we were able to infer an estimate for the last half of fiscal 1954, i.e. the first two quarters of calendar 1954. These estimates indicated a downward movement, which was assigned equally to the two quarters. In anticipation of slight further cuts in government purchases during the last two quarters of calendar 1954, we took as our basic 1954 estimate of government purchases 55.0 billion current dollars, the annual rate estimated for the second quarter of 1954. State and local governments' purchases of goods and services were extrapolated along their recent trend; total government purchases from abroad were cut 0.4 billion current dollars from their 1953 level of 3.4. These estimates gave our basic figure for $p_G 10^{-2} G$. Government payrolls, $p 10^{-2} W_2$, were assumed to constitute the same proportion of $p_G 10^{-2} G$ as they had in the reported first three quarters of 1953. The average annual earnings of government employees was extrapolated along its recent trend, enabling us to deduce the level of government employment N_G corresponding to a given level of $p 10^{-2} W_2$. Our alternative fiscal policies involved appropriate modifications of these central estimates.

---

[1]) U.S. Department of Commerce, *Survey of Current Business*, September 1953, p. 9.

141

APPENDIX II. THE TAX-TRANSFER FUNCTIONS

INTRODUCTION

In the statistical estimation of the parameters of the econometric model, the tax-transfer items, namely, the variables T, T_W, T_P, T_C and T_A, were treated as exogenous. They were given the same treatment in the making of the ex-post forecasts for 1951 and 1952 described in Chapter V. The assumption underlying such a procedure is that the values of these variables are set by political authorities and are not determined in the endogenous economic sphere. In fact, however, these variables refer to *yields*, while the political authority usually establishes a *rate* schedule, which operates upon the tax or transfer base (generally an endogenous variable) to determine, jointly with the other relationships, the tax or transfer yield.

Hence, a more realistic procedure would be to prepare tax-transfer *functions*, giving mathematical expression to tax-transfer legislation. This procedure, of course, becomes a necessary one when making ex-ante forecasts. To illustrate, we will sketch the method of deriving these functions in making the 1954 forecasts described in Chapter VI. The analogous work done in forecasting 1953 and in calculating two-year multipliers will be summarized briefly. In all three forecasting situations, the range of alternative tax-transfer legislative proposals being considered for the forecast period called for the preparation of corresponding, alternative, tax-transfer functions.

The yields and bases of tax and transfer legislation are written in terms of current dollar values, while our variables are in constant dollars. Hence, in estimating a linear corporate profit tax function, say, we first obtain it as

$$T_C^* = a_0 + a_1 P_C^*,$$

where the * denotes current dollar values. Then dividing through by $p10^{-2}$ we obtain the function in the form used for forecasting

$$T_C = \frac{a_0}{p10^{-2}} + a_1 P_C.$$

The scaling factor 10^{-2} is used to reduce p from a base of 100 to a base of 1.00.

FORECASTS FOR 1954

The range of alternatives for 1954 tax-transfer policy was indicated in discussing the forecasts for that year in Chapter VI. Since these alternatives differed with regard to several particular items of taxes, we derived separate functions for the various components of our tax-transfer variables, then modified these functions as we moved from one alternative policy to another. Where the tax alternative consisted of the continuation of a tax rate schedule which had been in force for two or three prior years, we fitted our functions to the observed values of the variables in those years. [1]) Where a rate schedule had been in force for only one period, we obtained additional observations on the schedule by adjusting, on the basis of various studies, the historical observations to a hypothetical level, viz. what they would have been if the present law had then been in effect. Where the tax alternative involved the modification of an existing tax rate schedule, we again constructed hypothetical observations by using the relationship between the existing and the modified law from which to derive our tax functions. As a rule, we did not use 1953 observations in deriving tax-transfer functions because of the preliminary nature of the 1953 data available at the time the forecasts were made.

INDIRECT TAXES LESS SUBSIDIES

Our variable T includes indirect business taxes, business transfer payments, current surplus of government enterprises minus subsidies, and the "statistical discrepancy" which equates the two independent measures (income side and expenditure side) of Gross National Product. We related indirect business taxes T_X to the overall level of activity and fitted a line to the 1951 and 1952 observations for the tax policies

---

[1]) The fitting procedure was not based on methods of statistical inference. In most cases, it involved fitting a straight line to two or three points by inspection.

which assumed continuation of the existing excise tax structure. The 1951 observation was first revised to allow for the fact that the existing excise tax law was not in effect throughout 1951. [1]) The resulting function for indirect business taxes was

(2.1.a) $\quad p10^{-2}T_X = 0.0924\, p10^{-2}(Y + T + D) - 4.084.$

For the other components of T we assumed a current dollar amount at 1952 levels or in accord with recent trends

(2.1.b)

Business Transfers	$= \quad 0.930$
Current Surplus Minus Subsidies	$= -0.100$
Statistical Discrepancy	$= \quad 0.500$

Adding up (2.1.a) and (2.1.b) and expressing the result in terms of constant dollars, we have the first indirect tax less subsidies function.

(2.1.c) $\qquad T = 0.0924(Y + T + D) - \dfrac{2.754}{p10^{-2}}.$

Our alternatives included two possible changes in the excise tax schedule. The first would occur if the rate increases of the 1951 act were allowed to expire on April 1. Such a return to the old rate structure was estimated by the U.S. Treasury Department [2]) to involve an *annual* revenue loss of about 1 billion current dollars or 0.750 for the April-December period. Since excise taxes are on particular commodities which may not move exactly with overall activity, and since the aggregative character of our variables does not permit the derivation of tax functions for individual commodities, we adopted the Treasury Department's estimate of the tax's revenue effect, and simply adjusted the constant of our indirect tax function, obtaining

(2.1.a′) $\quad p10^{-2}T_X = 0.0924\, p10^{-2}(Y + T + D) - 4.834.$

We combined this with (2.1.b), to obtain a second alternative indirect tax less subsidies function

(2.1.c′) $\qquad T = 0.0924(Y + T + D) - \dfrac{3.504}{p10^{-2}}.$

---

[1]) U.S. Treasury Department, Tax Advisory Staff of the Secretary, *The Revenue Act of 1951: A Summary*, mimeographed, Nov. 14, 1951, pp. 4–9.

[2]) Joint Committee on the Economic Report, *Federal Tax Changes and Estimated Revenue Losses Under Present Law*, Joint Committee Print, 82d Congress, 2d Session, p. 7.

We also considered a $ 1 billion current dollar *increase* in excise taxes, obtaining

(2.1.a") $\qquad p10^{-2}T_X = 0.0924\,p10^{-2}(Y + T + D) - 3.084,$

which, combined with (2.1.b), yielded a third indirect tax less subsidies function

(2.1.c") $\qquad T = 0.0924(Y + T + D) - \dfrac{1.754}{p10^{-2}}.$

TAXES LESS TRANSFERS ON WAGE INCOME

A major component of our variable T_W is the wage-earners' share of the federal personal income tax. The rate schedule for this tax differed in 1950, 1951, and 1952. The existing, 1953, structure was the same as that in 1952. Fortunately, a study by Joseph A. Pechman [1] had estimated what the total federal personal income tax yield would have been in each of the years 1948–53 had the existing (1952–1953) rate schedule been in effect. Allocating these hypothetical yields among wage, nonwage nonfarm, and farm income recipients in accordance with the procedure noted in Appendix I, page 116, and fitting a line to the 1950–53 observations, we obtained a linear relation between federal personal income taxes and wage income

(2.2.a) $\qquad p10^{-2}T_W^F = 0.1064\,p10^{-2}(W_1 + W_2) - 1.640.$

A second such function was constructed to describe the rate schedule which would go into effect if the scheduled January 1 rate reduction were made. The scheduled tax reduction was 10% throughout most of the income brackets, [2] with the exception of the highest, where relatively little wage income falls. Hence, reducing each of the 1950–53 yields by 10%, we fitted a second function for federal personal income tax on wage income

(2.2.a') $\qquad p10^{-2}T_W^F = 0.0958\,p10^{-2}(W_1 + W_2) - 1.490.$

In addition to this rate reduction, we also considered a general re-

---

[1] Joseph A. Pechman, "Yield of the Individual Income Tax During a Recession," *National Tax Journal*, Vol. VII, March, 1954, pp. 1–16. A preliminary draft of this study was made available to us at the time of forecasting.

[2] Joint Committee on the Economic Report, *op. cit.*, pp. 2, 3.

writing of the federal personal income tax law which would reduce 1954 revenues by 0.5 billion current dollars to be evenly divided between wage and nonwage nonfarm income recipients. Adjusting the constant term of our function, we obtained the third linear relation between federal personal income taxes and wage income

$$(2.2.a'') \qquad p10^{-2}T_W^F = 0.0958\ p10^{-2}(W_1 + W_2) - 1.240.$$

Contributions to the Old Age and Survivors Insurance system was the other component of T_W isolated for separate treatment because it was one of the fiscal policy elements up for legislative action. The existing law had been in effect since 1951, and by fitting a straight line to the 1951 and 1952 points we calculated the first OASI tax function

$$(2.2.b) \qquad p10^{-2}T_W^S = 0.0239\ p10^{-2}W_1 - 0.240.$$

Since government employees are not under OASI coverage, the tax base variable used was W_1.

Under terms of the law, an increase in the contribution rate from 3% to 4% was scheduled for January 1, 1954. In raising the observed 1951 and 1952 yields by one-third, we were led to a second OASI tax function

$$(2.2.b') \qquad p10^{-2}T_W^S = 0.0318\ p10^{-2}W_1 - 0.310.$$

Other contributions to social insurance were related to the total wage bill by a line fitted to the 1951 and 1952 observations

$$(2.2.c) \qquad p10^{-2}T_W^O = 0.0157\ p10^{-2}(W_1 + W_2) + 2.046.$$

Unemployment benefits (a transfer item) and state and local personal income taxes on wage recipients were grouped together, and related to the total wage bill by a line fitted to 1949–52 observations, yielding

$$(2.2.d) \qquad p10^{-2}T_W^U = -\ 0.0195\ p10^{-2}(W_1 + W_2) + 4.037.\ [1]$$

The other components of T_W, viz. other federal, state, and local transfer payments to wage recipients; business transfers; state and

---

[1] We considered relating unemployment benefits to the level of unemployment, $(N - N_W - N_E - N_F)$. However, this would have stepped up the nonlinearity of the forecasting equations to an inconvenient degree; instead we used the real wage bill as an (inverse) indicator of unemployment.

local personal income taxes on wage recipients; and miscellaneous taxes and "nontaxes" (e.g. licenses) on wage recipients were extrapolated on the basis of their recent trends, and summed together algebraically to yield the final T_W component, a net transfer item

$$(2.2.\text{e}) \qquad p10^{-2}T_W^M = 9.310.$$

Having estimated these component functions, we summed them into appropriate combinations, to represent the alternative fiscal policy packages considered in our 1954 forecasts, in accord with the definition

$$(2.2.\text{f}) \qquad T_W = T_W^F + T_W^S + T_W^O - T_W^U - T_W^M.$$

The last three components, expressed in (2.2.c), (2.2.d), and (2.2.e) respectively, were the same in all the fiscal policy packages considered. On adding (2.2.a'') and (2.2.b) to these, we obtained the single function

$$(2.2.\text{g}) \qquad T_W = 0.1549W_1 + 0.1310W_2 - \frac{13.981}{p10^{-2}}.$$

Substituting (2.2.a') and (2.2.b'), we get a second such function

$$(2.2.\text{h}) \qquad T_W = 0.1628W_1 + 0.1310W_2 - \frac{13.801}{p10^{-2}}.$$

Finally, substituting (2.2.a) and (2.2.b'), we get a third

$$(2.2.\text{i}) \qquad T_W = 0.1734W_1 + 0.1416W_2 - \frac{13.951}{p10^{-2}}.$$

CORPORATE INCOME AND EXCESS PROFITS TAXES

In the case of T_C, taxes on income and excess profits of corporations, we are faced with only a single tax item. However, a problem does arise because the concept of corporate profits embodied in our variable P_C differs in two major respects from that of the Bureau of Internal Revenue. P_C excludes inventory capital gains and is net of depreciation charged at replacement cost, while the tax base includes inventory capital gains and is net of depreciation charged at original cost. Hence, we first defined a variable $p10^{-2}\tilde{P}_C$ to be the corporate income tax base on the BIR concept, reported in the national accounts as corporate profits before inventory valuation adjustment. Using quarterly observations from the second quarter of 1951 through the second quarter of 1953, over which time the rate schedule was constant, we fitted the line

(2.3.a) $$p10^{-2}T_C = 0.635 \, p10^{-2}\tilde{P}_C - 4.134.$$

Then we extrapolated the corporate share of the revaluation of depreciation on the basis of its recent trend, assumed that there would be no net capital gains or losses on inventory in 1954 and obtained

(2.3.b) $$T_C = 0.635P_C + \frac{1.862}{p10^{-2}}.$$

We considered three proposed revisions in the corporate tax structure: 1) The scheduled January 1 removal of the excess profits tax provisions, 2) a reduction of the tax rate on ordinary profits from 52% to 47% as of April 1, and 3) rewriting of the provisions of the law with a resultant reduction in tax revenues of 0.5 billion current dollars. We had estimates of the excess profits tax yield in 1951 and 1952 and by deducting these from the total corporate tax yield, $p10^{-2}T_C$, obtained from the function (2.3.a) in these years, we obtained the yield of the ordinary profits tax. These yields for 1951 and 1952 were related to $p10^{-2}\tilde{P}_C$. After taking into account the depreciation adjustment, we obtained our second corporate profits tax function

(2.3.c) $$T_C = 0.4497P_C + \frac{5.982}{p10^{-2}}.$$

By adjusting the constant of (2.3.c), we calculated the function expressing the tax law with the rewriting of provisions in addition to the removal of the excess profits tax

(2.3.d) $$T_C = 0.4497P_C + \frac{5.482}{p10^{-2}}.$$

The five point reduction in the ordinary profits tax rate, effective for nine months of the year, amounted to a 7% reduction in the tax rate. Making this reduction in the ordinary profits tax yields for 1951 and 1952 described in the preceding paragraph, fitting a new line, and then making the replacement cost depreciation adjustment, we obtained another corporate profits tax function

(2.3.e) $$T_C = 0.418P_C + \frac{5.522}{p10^{-2}}.$$

As a matter of fact, this function was not employed in making 1954 forecasts. Instead, rewriting of provisions was considered together with the excess profits tax removal and reduction in ordinary profits tax rate. The function for this combination was obtained by adjusting the constant in (2.3.e) to obtain

$$(2.3.f) \qquad T_C = 0.418 P_C + \frac{5.022}{p10^{-2}}.$$

TAXES LESS TRANSFERS ON PERSONAL NONWAGE NONFARM INCOME

To facilitate our analysis in making 1954 forecasts we separated out the personal component P_N – entrepreneurial income, interest, rents, and corporate dividends – of our nonwage nonfarm income variable P

$$(2.4.a) \qquad P_N = P - P_C + (P_C - T_C - S_P) = P - T_C - S_P.$$

Accordingly, we separated out the corresponding component, T_N, of the tax variable T_P

$$(2.4.b) \qquad T_N = T_P - T_C.$$

First we derived a function for the federal personal income tax T_N^F on the corresponding income share. Our figure for federal personal income tax is on a collection basis. In the case of wage income, which is subject to tax withholding at source, the tax collections are appropriately related to current income. However, collections from nonwage income recipients are not withheld, and are only in part based on current period income, the remainder being on the liability incurred for income of the preceding period. The actual arrangement is such that during a year collections from nonwage income recipients consist of about half of their current year liability plus about half of their previous year liability.

Hence the procedure in obtaining the 1954 T_N^F function was as follows: Denote personal nonwage nonfarm income on the Bureau of Internal Revenue concept (i.e., before making the inventory valuation and replacement cost depreciation adjustments for entrepreneurial income) by $p10^{-2}\tilde{P}_N$. We had already determined what the personal income tax on such income would have been in the years 1950–1953 if the 1953 law had been in effect. Fitting a straight line to these points we obtained a function for the existing law

(2.4.c) $$p10^{-2}T_N^F = 0.539\,p10^{-2}\tilde{P}_N - 18.529.$$

Making the observed inventory valuation and replacement cost depreciation adjustments for 1953, we got the tax *liability* function on 1953 income

(2.4.d) $$\begin{aligned} p10^{-2}T_N^{F(53)} &= 0.539\,p_{53}10^{-2}(P_N)_{53} - 14.720 \\ &= 11.004. \end{aligned}$$

Assuming zero inventory valuation adjustment for 1954 and extrapolating the entrepreneurial replacement cost depreciation adjustment on the basis of its recent trend, we estimated the tax *liability* function on 1954 income if the existing rate schedule were continued

(2.4.e) $$p10^{-2}T_N^{F(54)} = 0.539\,p10^{-2}(P_N)_{54} - 14.217.$$

If the existing rate schedule were continued, federal personal income tax *collections* from nonwage nonfarm income recipients would be comprised of payment of half the liability of (2.4.d) plus half the liability of (2.4.e). We formed this sum to get the linear relation between federal personal income taxes and nonwage nonfarm income

(2.4.f) $$T_N^F = 0.269P_N - \frac{1.607}{p10^{-2}}.$$

On the other hand, if the scheduled January 1 cuts in the rate structure were made effective they would involve about an 8% reduction in the bracket rates when the smaller reduction in the rates of the upper brackets, in which some nonwage nonfarm income falls, are taken into account. We made this reduction and refitted a line to the 1950–53 data to get a new *liability* function for 1954 incomes, which, after inventory valuation and replacement cost depreciation adjustments, appeared as

(2.4.e') $$p10^{-2}T_N^{F(54)} = 0.496\,p10^{-2}(P_N)_{54} - 13.086.$$

Adding one-half this liability to one-half the liability on account of 1953 income (which would still be subject to 1953 rates), we found a second equation for federal personal income taxes on nonwage nonfarm income

(2.4.f') $$T_N^F = 0.248P_N - \frac{1.041}{p10^{-2}}.$$

As previously indicated, in addition to this rate reduction we also considered a general rewriting of provisions of the federal personal income tax law which would reduce revenues by 0.25 billion current dollars from nonwage nonfarm income recipients. Adjusting the constant term of our function, we obtained a third equation expressed in constant dollars as

$$(2.4.f'') \qquad T_N^F = 0.248 P_N - \frac{1.291}{p10^{-2}}.$$

We extrapolated the other items of taxes and transfers on personal nonwage nonfarm income on the basis of recent trends; they amounted to a net transfer item

$$(2.4.g) \qquad T_N^M = \frac{2.950}{p10^{-2}}.$$

Having estimated these two component functions, we formed three combinations in accord with the definition

$$(2.4.h) \qquad T_N = T_N^F - T_N^M$$

to represent the three alternative fiscal policies considered in our 1954 forecasts. For the policy envisaging continuation of the 1953 federal personal income tax schedule, we added (2.4.f) and (2.4.g), obtaining

$$(2.4.i) \qquad T_N = 0.269 P_N - \frac{4.557}{p10^{-2}}.$$

For the policy envisaging the scheduled cuts in the federal personal income tax schedule, we added (2.4.f') and (2.4.g), obtaining

$$(2.4.j) \qquad T_N = 0.248 P_N - \frac{3.991}{p10^{-2}}.$$

For the policy envisaging the rewriting of provisions in addition to the scheduled cuts in the tax schedule, we added (2.4.f'') and (2.4.g), obtaining

$$(2.4.k) \qquad T_N = 0.248 P_N - \frac{4.241}{p10^{-2}}.$$

TAXES LESS TRANSFERS ON FARM INCOME

In the case of farm income recipients, we did not construct detailed functions, nor did we consider the impacts of alternative fiscal policies. Instead we simply extrapolated, on the basis of recent trends, the current dollar net tax-transfer on farm income

$$(2.5.a) \qquad\qquad T_A = \frac{0.500}{p10^{-2}}.$$

The justification of this procedure lies in the low magnitude of the item and its approximate invariance under alternative policies; the precise variation in the level of disposable farm income under those alternative fiscal policies which we consider would not induce any significant change in the level of the other variables.

Forecasts for 1953

In constructing the tax-transfer functions for forecasting 1953 economic activity as described in Chapter V, we had used the same general method as in the preceding section. However, we considered alternatives for only two aspects of tax-transfer policy – the corporate excess profits tax and the federal personal income tax. Hence, we did not decompose our variables T, T_W, T_P, T_C and T_A but rather determined functions for these five variables directly. We will briefly describe how these functions were determined; our experience with the 1953 forecasts suggested some modifications incorporated into the procedures by which the 1954 functions were constructed.

Indirect Taxes less Subsidies

We related indirect taxes, business transfers, and current surplus of government enterprises less subsidies to the overall level of activity, assumed the national accounts' statistical discrepancy to be zero, and fitted a line to the 1951 and 1952 observations. Expressed in constant dollars, we obtained the function

$$(2.6.a) \qquad T = 0.1185(Y + T + D) - \frac{12.356}{p10^{-2}}.$$

Taxes less Transfers on Wage Income

For the policy which involved no change in federal personal income tax rates, we fitted a line to the 1951 and 1952 observations on the total taxes less transfers on wage income. This yielded our first function

$$(2.7.a) \qquad T_W = 0.24(W_1 + W_2) - \frac{28.902}{p10^{-2}}.$$

For the policy envisaging a 10 percent annual cut in the federal personal income tax, effective July 1, 1953, we reduced the observed levels of this tax by 5% and fitted a new function to the 1951 and 1952 observations. This yielded our second function

$$(2.7.b) \qquad T_W = 0.2286(W_1 + W_2) - \frac{27.671}{p10^{-2}}.$$

Corporate Income and Excess Profits Taxes

We fitted a straight line to the seasonally adjusted quarterly observations for 1952 on corporate income and excess profits taxes and corporate profits (Bureau of Internal Revenue concept). Then, assuming zero inventory capital gains for 1953 and extrapolating the replacement cost depreciation adjustment according to its recent trend, we converted this function to a relation between corporate taxes and corporate profits (our concept). This yielded our first function

$$(2.8.a) \qquad T_C = 0.685P_C + \frac{1.662}{p10^{-2}}.$$

At this point, the only estimate we had available on the yield of the excess profits tax was that it amounted to some 3 billion current dollars annually. Hence, for the policy envisaging a mid-year removal of the tax, we adjusted the constant of (2.8.a) and obtained our second function

$$(2.8.b) \qquad T_C = 0.685P_C + \frac{0.162}{p10^{-2}}.$$

Taxes less Transfers on Nonwage Nonfarm Income

We fitted a line to the 1951 and 1952 observations on taxes less transfers on nonwage nonfarm income and total nonwage nonfarm income (with corporate and entrepreneurial income on BIR concept).

153

Then assuming zero capital gains on inventory and extrapolating the replacement cost depreciation adjustment, we obtained our first function

$$(2.9.a) \qquad T_P = 0.2593P + \frac{12.933}{p10^{-2}}.$$

For the policy involving the mid-year removal of the excess profits tax, we adjusted the constant of (2.9.a), obtaining our second function

$$(2.9.b) \qquad T_P = 0.2593P + \frac{11.433}{p10^{-2}}.$$

For the policy which envisaged a 10% annual cut (effective for half of 1953) in the federal personal income tax, in addition to the mid-year removal of the excess profits tax, we reduced the observed federal personal income tax yields by 5% and fitted a new line to the 1951 and 1952 data. Expressed in constant dollars, after the replacement cost depreciation adjustment was made, our third function was

$$(2.9.c) \qquad T_P = 0.243P + \frac{12.032}{p10^{-2}}.$$

TAXES LESS TRANSFERS ON FARM INCOME

We simply extrapolated the current dollar net tax-transfer item on farm income:

$$(2.10.a) \qquad T_A = \frac{0.750}{p10^{-2}}.$$

Allowing for the 10% annual reduction in the federal personal income tax, effective for half of 1953, we estimated the alternative

$$(2.10.b) \qquad T_A = \frac{0.710}{p10^{-2}}.$$

TAX-TRANSFER FUNCTIONS FOR CALCULATION OF TWO-YEAR MULTIPLIERS

As described in Chapter VI, after making the alternative forecasts for 1954, we compared the effects of allowing two of the fiscal policies to run for an additional year. The tax-transfer functions were identical under these two policies, and we considered their continuation for an additional year. However, two modifications were necessary. The replacement cost depreciation adjustment had to be extrapolated for another year, with zero inventory capital gains again being assumed. Also because of the lag in the T_N function (collections of federal personal income tax from nonwage nonfarm income recipients being in part based on the previous period's income, which differed between the two policies) the policies had different T_N functions in the second year. We list the tax-transfer functions for the second year.

$$T_W = 0.1549W_1 + 0.1310W_2 - \frac{13.981}{p10^{-2}},$$

$$T_C = 0.4497P_C + \frac{7.016}{p10^{-2}},$$

$$T_N = 0.248P_N - \frac{1.788}{p10^{-2}} \quad \text{(Variant I),}$$

$$T_N = 0.248P_N - \frac{1.316}{p10^{-2}} \quad \text{(Variant V),}$$

$$T_A = -\frac{0.500}{p10^{-2}},$$

$$T = 0.0924(Y + T + D) - \frac{2.754}{p10^{-2}}.$$

APPENDIX III. RESIDUALS FROM ESTIMATED EQUATIONS

ANNUAL RESIDUALS FROM STRUCTURAL EQUATIONS
Original Model

Year	Equation Number						
	1	2	3	4	5	6	7
1929	1.50	5.0	−0.32	−1.06	−2.03	0.25	0.34
1930	−0.32	−1.8	−0.34	−0.83	−2.41	−0.26	−0.76
1931	−0.37	−2.1	−0.04	−1.10	−2.04	0.23	0.88
1932	−0.58	−3.7	0.42	−0.58	−2.09	−0.17	0.91
1933	−0.22	0.2	0.39	0.01	−1.10	0.42	−1.58
1934	0.74	1.5	0.09	0.64	0.55	1.16	−1.21
1935	−0.16	1.4	0.26	0.72	0.01	0.14	−1.44
1936	0.15	0.3	−1.19	0.35	0.84	−0.11	−1.67
1937	−0.58	1.0	−0.50	0.41	0.35	0.83	−2.68
1938	−0.24	−5.4	0.70	−0.15	0.35	−1.45	4.12
1939	0.65	−0.6	−0.23	−0.22	0.58	−0.17	1.89
1940	−0.24	1.3	0.04	0.30	0.49	−1.09	2.24
1941	−0.54	2.4	−0.03	0.70	−0.02	−1.08	3.32
1946	−0.35	−2.0	−0.05	−1.74	0.83	−0.60	−1.10
1947	0.54	−1.0	0.18	0.55	1.97	1.22	−4.19
1948	−1.07	3.4	0.52	0.61	1.12	0.50	−1.88
1949	0.56	−3.8	0.48	0.54	1.04	−0.54	−0.71
1950	0.51	4.0	−0.37	0.86	1.57	0.72	3.53

Year	Equation Number						
	8	9	10	12 ¹)	13	14	15
1929	−1.13	0.8	−0.66	−0.054	1.7	−0.37	15.2
1930	1.24	0.1	−0.21	−0.057	0.0	−0.39	−43.8
1931	−2.37	−0.2	−0.60	0.088	−3.6	−0.09	−30.8
1932	1.25	−0.5	0.21	0.221	0.4	0.56	3.6
1933	−4.16	−0.3	0.29	0.141	−0.6	0.46	−30.6
1934	10.20	−0.4	−0.71	0.049	2.2	−0.25	−24.0
1935	−3.72	0.1	1.66	−0.016	0.7	−0.28	−4.8
1936	−3.03	0.1	−1.13	−0.092	0.2	−0.19	15.3
1937	6.42	0.6	1.26	−0.081	−1.3	0.19	28.7
1938	2.04	−0.4	0.86	−0.019	−1.0	0.79	−2.7
1939	−7.43	−0.1	−0.52	−0.060	−0.4	0.53	−10.3
1940	−3.29	0.1	−0.27	−0.094	0.9	0.29	14.7
1941	−0.16	−0.3	−0.13	−0.139	1.1	0.14	11.8
1946	7.39	0.2	1.87	−0.011	−0.3	−0.36	0.5
1947	4.26	−0.4	1.69	0.017	0.7	−0.28	23.6
1948	0.37	−0.2	1.04	0.073	−0.3	−0.08	36.0
1949	−8.08	−0.1	−1.84	0.040	−0.3	−0.24	−1.1
1950	0.17	0.9	−2.82	−0.005	−0.1	−0.44	−5.8

¹) These are the residuals from the logarithmic form of the equation.

Re-Estimated Model

Year	Equation Number						
	1*	2*	3*	4*	5*	6*	7*
1929	1.71	4.1	0.02	−1.00	−1.31	1.69	0.84
1930	−0.88	−3.0	−0.54	−0.88	−1.24	−0.41	−1.20
1931	−0.76	−3.2	−0.74	−1.33	−0.69	−0.24	0.28
1932	−1.23	−4.5	−0.43	−1.01	−0.55	−1.63	0.29
1933	−0.58	0.1	−0.14	−0.44	0.18	0.03	−2.41
1934	0.37	1.9	0.00	0.30	1.31	1.22	−0.67
1935	0.00	2.1	0.28	0.50	0.33	0.21	−0.80
1936	0.32	1.1	−1.09	0.26	0.71	0.59	−1.13
1937	−0.20	1.7	−0.90	0.34	0.06	0.84	−1.40
1938	−0.15	−4.9	0.14	−0.25	0.30	−2.40	3.57
1939	0.70	0.1	−0.11	−0.23	0.20	0.14	1.95
1940	0.83	1.8	0.18	0.33	−0.17	−0.83	2.91
1941	0.01	2.6	0.01	0.93	−0.59	0.14	3.85
1946	−1.03	−2.3	−0.02	−1.45	−0.75	−1.17	−1.55
1947	0.50	−1.9	0.34	0.77	0.47	1.36	−5.18
1948	−0.39	2.1	1.11	1.05	−0.26	0.74	−3.61
1949	1.40	−5.6	1.03	0.42	0.23	−1.46	−1.29
1950	1.67	3.5	0.10	0.56	0.53	0.68	2.23
1951	−1.89	3.6	0.32	0.86	−0.07	0.16	2.31
1952	−0.44	1.1	0.43	0.28	1.30	0.35	1.00

Year	Equation Number							
	8*	9*	10*	11*	12* [1])	13*	14*	15*
1929	−1.16	0.3	−0.32	6.7	−0.067	2.9	−0.34	10.6
1930	1.14	−0.4	−0.88	− 6.6	−0.065	−0.2	−0.37	−48.2
1931	−2.61	−0.4	−1.37	−20.4	0.077	−3.2	−0.06	−35.1
1932	0.73	−0.5	−1.88	−19.3	0.222	0.8	0.62	0.3
1933	−4.65	0.0	−1.03	− 5.2	0.132	0.3	0.45	−32.7
1934	10.04	−0.2	−1.27	4.6	0.036	2.0	−0.32	−23.7
1935	−3.54	0.4	0.87	19.5	−0.020	0.5	−0.27	− 3.6
1936	−2.89	0.1	−0.16	23.1	−0.093	−0.2	−0.17	15.6
1937	6.50	0.4	0.87	20.9	−0.085	−1.6	0.19	26.1
1938	2.22	−0.9	0.01	− 0.9	−0.022	−1.4	0.82	− 3.7
1939	−7.43	0.1	−0.15	− 0.8	−0.070	−0.9	0.59	−10.0
1940	−3.21	0.1	0.40	0.7	−0.103	0.5	0.36	15.7
1941	0.05	0.2	1.51	6.2	−0.141	0.5	0.21	11.8
1946	7.73	−0.6	1.29	23.2	−0.016	0.0	−0.28	0.9
1947	4.92	−0.1	1.00	29.1	0.014	0.5	−0.21	19.5
1948	1.21	0.4	1.58	12.2	0.064	−0.1	−0.01	31.8
1949	−4.99	−0.1	−0.25	−23.0	0.030	−0.2	−0.17	− 5.3
1950	−2.27	0.7	0.03	−25.7	−0.017	0.2	−0.37	−10.0
1951	5.51	0.0	−0.06	− 9.0	0.040	1.1	−0.35	41.1
1952	−7.30	0.4	−0.20	−35.3	0.084	−1.5	−0.31	− 1.4

[1]) These are the residuals from the logarithmic form of the equation.

INDEX

Accounting identities, 31–33, 53, 92.

Agricultural and nonagricultural prices, estimates of relation between, 92, 105, formulation of relation between, 22-23, *see also* Parity policy.

Agricultural income, measurement of, 89–90.

Agricultural income determination equation, discussion of estimates of, 69–70, estimates of, 52, 63, 92, 104, formulation of, 20–22.

Arden, Bruce, xi.

Autoregressive transformations, in forecasting, 76–77, *see also* Serial correlation.

Barger, H., 116, 118, 119, 120, 124, 126, 127.

Brown, A. J., 25.

Brown, T. M., 2, 7, 8.

Bureau of Agricultural Economics, United States, 126, 127, *see also* Department of Agriculture, United States.

Bureau of Internal Revenue, United States, 147, 149, 153, *see also* Department of the Treasury, United States.

Canada, econometric models of, 2, 7.

Capital, stock of, 117, stock of in depreciation equation, 15-16, stock of in investment equation, 11, 68, stock of in production function, 69.

Capital consumption allowances, 115-16, 138, *see also* Depreciation.

Christ, C., 2.

Clark, Colin, 128.

Cobb, C., 16.

Computation, high-speed methods, 3, 70–71, limited information estimates, 47–50.

Constant dollar gross national product, 115, 137.

Consumer surveys, 1953 forecast, 87, *see also* Surveys of Consumer Finances.

Consumption equation, discussion of estimates of, 57–66, estimates of, 51, 54, 90, 93, formulation of, 4–10.

Corporate income taxes, 1953 forecast, 153, 1954 forecast, 103, 147–49, *see also* Excess profits taxes.

Corporate profits and nonwage nonfarm income, discussion of estimates of relation between, 68–69, estimates of relation between, 52, 57, 91, 96, formulation of relation between, 14-15.

Corporate savings equation, estimates of, 51, 56, 91, 95, formulation of, 13–14.

Council of Economic Advisers, 134, 135, 137.

Cowles Commission, 1, 2, 3.

Definition equations, 31–33, 53, 92.

Demand for labor equation,

estimates of, 52, 59, 91, 98,
   formulation of, 16–17.
Department of Agriculture, United
   States, 135, 140,
   see also Bureau of Agricultural Economics, United States.
Department of Commerce, United
   States, vii, 2–3, 7, 115, 116, 124–28,
   134–41.
Department of Labor, United States,
   137.
Department of the Treasury, United
   States, 128, 144,
   see also Bureau of Internal Revenue,
   United States.
Depreciation, 115–16, 138,
   accounting records, 15,
   in investment equation, 12,
   revaluation of, 16.
Depreciation equation,
   discussion of estimates of, 68–69,
   estimates of, 52, 58, 91, 97,
   formulation of, 15–16.
Disposable income, 7, 12, 13, 19, 116.
Distribution of income, in consumption
   equation, 4–7.
Disturbance, treatment of in forecasts, 75
   see also Residuals.
Dividends, in corporate savings
   equation, 14.
Dobrovolsky, S. P., 14.
Douglas, P. H., 16.
Durand, D., 28.

Endogenous variables, 34–35, 43–48,
   1951–52 extrapolations, 81,
   1953 forecasts, 85, 88,
   1954 forecast, 111,
   realization of forecast 1954, ix.
Engel curves, 4.
Estimation, statistical,
   numerical values of coefficients, 50–
   53, 90–92,
   principles of, 42–50.

Ex-ante forecasts, 72–73,
   1953, 82–88,
   1954, 95–112.
Excess profits taxes,
   1953 forecast, 84–86, 153,
   1954 forecast, 96–103, 147–49.
Excess reserves, in money market adjustment equation, 29.
Exogenous variables, 35–36, 43–48,
   see also Predetermined variables.
Ex-post extrapolations, 72,
   1951–52, 78–82.
External information, use of in forecasting, 77–78.
Extrapolation, data used in, 133–41.

Federal Home Loan Board, 130.
Federal Reserve Bank of New York,
   128–29, 140.
Federal Reserve Board, 117, 129–31,
   support of bond prices, 30.
Forecast,
   data used in, 133–41,
   1953, 82–88,
   1954, 95–112,
   1954 realization of, ix-x.
Forecast error, theory of, 74–75.
Forecasting, principles of, 72,
   treatment of government expenditures and taxes, 36–40,
   treatment of interest rate and money
   market equations, 40–41.
Fox, K., xi, 21.
Frane, Lenore, xi, 7, 116.
Friend, I., xi, 117, 129, 130.

Garvy, G., 129.
Goldenweiser, E. A., 129.
Goldsmith, R. W., xi, 117, 121, 126, 130.
Government expenditures,
   assumptions in 1953 forecasts, 135,
   assumptions in 1954 forecast, 103, 141,
   choice between current and constant
   dollar magnitudes, 36–38,
   treatment of in *ex-post* forecasts, 79.

Gross national product, accounting identity, 32–33,
see also Constant dollar gross national product *and* National accounts.

Hood, W. C., 42.

Idle cash balances, 25–26.
Implicit price deflator, 115, 137.
Import demand equation,
  estimates of, 52, 62, 91, 102,
  formulation of, 19.
Imports, measurement of, 89.
Indirect taxes,
  1953 forecast, 152,
  1954 forecast, 143–45.
Intercorrelation,
  in consumption equation, 57, 65,
  in import demand equation, 19–20.
Interest rate, in investment equation,
  11, 12, 67–68,
  in liquidity preference equation, 24, 27,
  in two-year extrapolation, 113.
Investment equation,
  discussion of estimates of, 66–68,
  estimates of, 51, 55, 90, 94,
  formulation of, 10–13.

Jaszi, G., xi.
Jones, Homer, xi.

Kalecki, M., 5, 29.
Keynes, J. M., 10, 11, 24, 25.
Keynesian economics, 2, 4, 8, 24–26.
Kisselgoff, A., 22, 28.
Klein, L. R., 1, 6, 7, 8, 42, 49, 60, 116.
Koopmans, T. C., 42.
Kuznets, S., 116, 118, 119.

Labor demand equation,
  estimates of, 52, 59, 91, 98,
  formulation of, 16-17.
Labor input, in production function, 17, 69.

Labor market adjustment equation,
  estimates of, 52, 61, 91, 101,
  formulation of, 18–19.
Labor's share, 17.
Lag,
  between investment and profits, 66–68, 85–86,
  between long- and short-term interest rate, 28–29,
  between wages and prices, 18,
  in consumption equation, 8, 62.
Least-squares estimates, 49–50.
Lewis, R. E., 129.
Limited information maximum likelihood, 44, 46.
Liquid assets, 117,
  in consumption equation, 8, 65,
  in forecasts, 41, 113, 140,
  in investment equation, 13, 68.
Liquidity preference equation, business,
  discussion of estimates of, 70,
  estimates of, 53, 65, 92, 108,
  formulation of, 26–28.
Liquidity preference equation, household,
  discussion of estimates of, 70,
  estimates of, 53, 64, 92, 107,
  formulation of, 23–26.
Long-run marginal propensity to consume, 63–64.
Long-term and short-term interest rates,
  estimates of relation between, 53, 66, 92, 109,
  formulation of relation between, 28.
Long-term interest rate, in liquidity preference equation, 24, 70.
Lutz, F., 130.

Man hours, in production function, 17.
Marginal efficiency of capital, 11.
Marginal propensity to consume or to save, 6, 58–64.
Margolis, J., 6.

163

Maximum likelihood, 44, 75.
Money illusion, 18.
Money market adjustment equation,
    estimates of, 53, 67, 92, 110,
    formulation of, 29–31.
Moody's total corporate bond yield, 129.
Morgan, J. N., 6.
Multiplier, 85, 104, 111–14.
Musgrave, R. A., xi, 135, 136.

National accounts, vii, 2–3, 115–16, 124–
    28, 134, 136.
National City Bank of New York, 138.
National income, accounting identity,
    32–33,
    see also National accounts.
Nonlinearities, 37, 40, 75.
Nonwage income, in investment
    equation, 11, 68,
    see also Corporate profits and nonwage
    nonfarm income.

Old Age and Survivors Insurance
    payments, 1954 forecast, 146.

Parity policy, 106,
    see also Agricultural and nonagri-
    cultural prices.
Pechman, J. A., 145.
Population, size of as variable in con-
    sumption equation, 9, 65.
Predetermined variables, 48–51,
    in forecasts, x, 73, 99,
    see also Exogenous variables.
Prediction, principles of, 72,
    see also Forecast error, and Fore-
    casting.
Price supports, in agriculture, 21, 22,
    see also Agricultural and nonagri-
    cultural prices.
Prices, determination of, 41,
    in liquidity preference equation, 27.
Probability density, 43–44.
Production function,

discussion of estimates of, 69,
    estimates of, 52, 60, 91, 100,
    formulation of, 17–18.
Productivity, trend of, x, 69.
Profits, in corporate savings equation,
    14,
    in investment equation, 11,
    see also Nonwage income.

Reduced forms of structural system, 44–
    46.
Relative prices, in agricultural income
    determination equation, 21, 69,
    in import demand equation, 19–20.
Residuals, 156–59,
    1948–52, 86, 106,
    1949–54, vii–viii,
    money market equations 1948–53,
    113.
Restrictions on structural system, 44–47.
Returns to scale, 69.
Revision of model, 89–95.

Serial correlation, 53,
    in forecasting, 75–76.
Shapiro, S., 117, 130.
Short-run marginal propensity to con-
    sume, 62–63.
Short-run multipliers, 85.
Short-term and long-term interest rates,
    estimation of relation between, 53, 66,
    92, 109,
    formulation of relation between, 28.
Short-term interest rate, in liquidity
    preference equation, 27.
Single-equation, least-squares estimates,
    49–50.
Speculative demand for cash, 24, 27.
Standard error of forecast, 74–75.
Stock of capital, 117,
    in depreciation equation, 15–16,
    in investment equation, 11, 68,
    in production function, 69.
Supply and demand, law of, 18, 29.

Surplus, in corporate savings equation, 13–14.
Surveys of Consumer Finances, 5, 6, 8, 57.

Taxation, choice between total collections and rates, 36–40,
forecast 1953 and 1954, 142–55,
forecast 1953, farm income, 154,
forecast 1954, farm income, 151–52,
forecast 1953, nonwage nonfarm income, 153–54,
forecast 1954, nonwage nonfarm income, 149–51,
forecast 1953, wage income, 152–53,
forecast 1954, wage income, 145–47,
treatment of in *ex-ante* forecasts, 83–84,
treatment of in *ex-post* extrapolations, 79, 142,

treatment of in two-year multipliers, 154–55.
Tinbergen, J., 1, 7, 13, 14.
Tobin, J., 25.
Transactions demand for cash, 24–25, 27–28, 70.
Transfer payments, forecasts 1953 and 1954, 142–55,
treatment of in *ex-post* forecasts, 142, *see also* Taxation.

Unemployment, in labor market adjustment equation, 18.
Unemployment benefits, 1954 forecast, 146.

Valavanis-Vail, S., xi, 35.

Wage bargaining, 18.
Wage-price lag, 18.
Wealth, in consumption equation, 8–9.